FOLLOW ME

A Study in Discipleship

ROBERT GRIFFITH

GRACE AND TRUTH PUBLISHING
PO Box 338, Gunnedah NSW 2380 Australia
www.graceandtruthpublishing.com.au

All Bible quotes are from the New International Version (NIV) expect where
otherwise stated.

NEW INTERNATIONAL VERSION (NIV), Copyright 1973, 1978 and 1984 by
international Bible Society. Used by permission of Zondervan Publishing House.
All rights reserved.

Other version quotes are from:

AMPLIFIED BIBLE (AMP), Copyright © 1954, 1958, 1962, 1964, 1965, 1987 by
The Lockman Foundation. Used by permission.

ENGLISH STANDARD VERSION (ESV), Copyright © 2001 by Crossway Bibles,
a division of Good News Publishers. Used by permission. All rights reserved.

NEW AMERICAN STANDARD BIBLE (NASB), Copyright © 1960, 1962, 1963, 1968,
1971, 1972, 1973, 1975, 1977, by The Lockman Foundation. Used by permission.

NEW KING JAMES VERSION (NKJV), Copyright © 1979, 1980, 1982, by Thomas
Nelson Inc. Used by permission. All rights reserved.

THE MESSAGE (MSG), by Eugene Peterson, Copyright © 1993, 1994, 1995, 1996,
and 2000. Used by permission of NavPress Publishing Group. All rights reserved.

REVISED STANDARD VERSION (RSV), Copyright © 1973, by Thomas Nelson Inc.
Used by permission. All rights reserved.

Quotes in square brackets are the author's comment.

ISBN 978-1-7635504-3-8

TABLE OF CONTENTS

1. INTRODUCTION

What does it really mean to follow Jesus? It's essential that we are rooted and grounded in God's love and that we understand His grace - the heart and soul of the gospel - but what about the daily struggle to live as a faithful disciple of Jesus? What about the real world of disappointments, trials, unrealised expectations and the very dark times when God seems so far away?

When Jesus stood by the lake that day and said, *"Follow me"*… where was He going? Well, we know now that He was going to Calvary!

If being a disciple of Jesus means participating in His life and embracing His ministry and the reality that He experienced, then there will be many challenges for those of us who desire to take His call to discipleship seriously.

We can continue to sit in the stands and be a spectator, saying all the right things; mixing with those in the game and even wearing the same uniform; believing we are actually involved in the real stuff; or we can be honest enough to admit that we are still in spiritual nappies, drinking spiritual milk and we have yet to taste the real meat of discipleship.

We may follow Jesus to the Mount of Transfiguration; we may follow Him as He heals the sick and raises the dead and casts out demons and rides triumphant into Jerusalem. But will we follow Him into Gethsemane yet? Will we share His heartache as Judas kisses Him on the cheek? Have we known His pain as His best friend disowns him in His hour of greatest need? Have we followed Him to that cold windy hill of death?

The discipleship road has many turns, potholes, speed humps and obstacles. There are tests at every bend and we often go through these tests many times throughout our earthly journey. The key question is this: are we prepared to embrace that journey with determination and conviction - ready to face anything that comes our way – and confident that whatever lies ahead on that road is under the total control of our Sovereign Lord?

Are we prepared to grow up spiritually; to mature in Christ; to digest the real meat of discipleship and not keep re-heating the same old milk? I want us to be brutally honest with ourselves here and let the Spirit of God examine our hearts and our lives and be prepared to admit that on the road of discipleship we may have a long way to go in our understanding of what it means to truly follow Jesus. So, as we prepare for this study in discipleship let's begin with a pretty confronting, but incredibly important passage from the book of Hebrews.

> **Hebrews 5:11-6:3** *"We have much to say about this, but it is hard to make it clear to you because you no longer try to understand. In fact, though by this time you ought to be teachers, you need someone to teach you the elementary truths of God's word all over again. You need milk, not solid food! Anyone who lives on milk, being still an infant, is not acquainted with the teaching about righteousness. But solid food is for the mature, who by constant use have trained themselves to distinguish good from evil.*
>
> *Therefore, let us move beyond the elementary teachings about Christ and be taken forward to maturity, not laying again the foundation of repentance from acts that lead to death, and of faith in God, instruction about cleansing rites, the laying on of hands, the resurrection of the dead, and eternal judgment. And God permitting, we will do so."*

Before I continue, let me warn you. It is not possible to discuss true what discipleship and following Jesus is all about without exposing the huge chasm between genuine discipleship and what most of us have experienced and observed in our lifetime. That means there will be many face-slapping observations and exhortations in this chapter and this whole book. So, brace yourself. But let me qualify the warning.

Firstly, I stand side by side with you as those confronting truths challenge us all. Every genuine preacher, teacher and writer has already been confronted by God through every word they write before they share that pain with others!

Secondly, I will never target individuals or local issues and so you never have to wonder, *"Is he talking about her, or what happened last week or that problem in my Church."* The answer is no, but of course the Holy Spirit may have real issues and people in mind as he speaks through my words.

Thirdly, you need to remember that my teaching is now reaching thousands of people each week in many different countries and so I am addressing the whole church and it is up to the hearers and the Holy Spirit to work out what applies to whom. In colloquial terms, 'If the cap fits, wear it' and let God change you; if it doesn't, let that statement sail past you to someone else. So, just relax, open your heart and mind to God and take on board whatever He intends.

So, from our Hebrews passage, we have to understand that it is entirely possible for us to stay a child forever, in spiritual terms. We can come to church, get involved in programs and ministries and yet never really grow at all. I want us to examine the modern church - not just my local fellowship - but the whole church as we know it today.

I believe we need to face the possibility that too many of those who sit in worship centres every single week, have not tasted the real meat of discipleship.

One example of our spiritual childhood that comes to mind is our prayers - they never seem to change for many of us. You would think that if a person was growing in their relationship with the Lord, they would pray differently from when they first embraced the gift of Salvation in Christ. But often that is not the case.

Another evidence of our immaturity is the division in the church. Paul told the Corinthians that their clinging to Peter, Apollos and himself was a sign of their spiritual immaturity. The Corinthians weren't fighting each other. They were just aligning themselves to different preachers.

At least they stayed in the same congregation. In our day we don't do that very well. We belong to different groups and meet in different buildings and speak against each other.

Instead of getting better ... many of Christ's followers are getting worse. For so many people today it seems so easy for them to walk out of one fellowship into another and take all their baggage and critical spirit and unresolved problems with them. They are often welcomed with open arms at the new place where no one holds them accountable for their actions.

Then if the new crowd doesn't do church the way they like it, they just move again, or they might even start their own version of church. The Body of Christ has never been so fragmented. At the last count there are over 48,000 separate denominations now, all claiming to be the Church Jesus promised to build! This is a sure sign of our spiritual infancy.

Another evidence of our immaturity is the obsession with *getting* and our resistance to *giving*. Too often we are just like little children, constantly wanting the Lord to help us, do this for us, give us that, make us well, make us happy, give us money. Some people just never stop begging. Like children, we do not know how to value the things we have. So often we ask for the wrong things. Isn't it interesting how many Christians are always more intrigued with the *gifts* of the Spirit than with the *fruit* of the Spirit?

When someone with a healing ministry comes to town, the church is never so packed. Children love the spectacular - but only the mature are interested in being trained in the school of love, joy, peace, patience, kindness, goodness, faithfulness, gentleness and self-control. If you offer a little child a $100 note or a bag of lollies - he'll probably take the bag of lollies.

We are the same way when it comes to materialism. We always go for the nice home, the new car, the big bank account, rather than spiritual things, because we don't have a mature value system.

We even try to use God to get these things. It's not enough to seek after material prosperity ourselves, we try to coax God into helping us get it! At times we can be a lot like selfish little children.

Another evidence of our spiritual immaturity is the lack of workers in the church. We have people who have been Christians for decades and still have no active ministry and have never even tried to lead a person to Christ. Their grand achievement may have been to invite someone to a meeting. If the person comes - they have done their duty - it's up to the Pastor now to preach the gospel, lead the person to Christ, baptise them and care for them from then on.

Every Sunday in many churches all over the world the gospel is preached. People respond and we put them in a newcomer's group to learn about the church, baptism and other fundamentals. But where do they go from there? By the time they finish that introduction to Christianity, we are off starting another newcomer's group, leaving them with no mentor to guide them into maturity.

No wonder our churches loses more people than we keep. No wonder the results of our big campaigns seem to shrink. The new believers - to put it bluntly - get bored with church as it has become in so many places today. The people are often told that they must grow and mature in Christ, but how can they if they are never fed anything but milk? Milk is good for a while; milk is all we can handle at first; but sooner or later if we don't get some solid food, we shrivel up and become malnourished and weak.

Everyone is to blame for this - Pastors, Theological Colleges and the people in churches who seem happy to drink milk all their lives. We can all become complacent and apathetic and so we shouldn't try to point the finger at anyone. We can all become victims of the structure in which we have been brought up. We cannot flee from that structure; it is woven into us, but we can make ourselves stop and think about what we are doing.

If we don't stop our ceaseless round of activities and ask God whether He is actually in any of those activities, then we are all guilty of contributing to the immaturity of the church today.

I spend a lot of time researching what God is doing across the church in our nation and around the world and I have to say that I have been shocked to see how little meat there is in the teaching and preaching of today.

The vast majority of people across most denominations are being fed the 'elementary things' referred to our Hebrews passage. This teaching is essential and foundational. That's why it is so important; that's why we need to make sure everyone has been exposed to it. But it must then be built upon. It is rich, wholesome milk, full of spiritual nutrients, but the meat comes when we move on into the real world around us and start to live it and grow in it.

To use another analogy, you cannot live on a foundation, no matter how strong it is or how flashy it looks. You have to build the house! When a builder pours a concrete slab, he waits for the slab to cure and reach sufficient strength and then he constructs the intended building on that slab. How pointless would it be for him to knock off when the slab is laid and move to the next job? For too many Christians around the world, that is their stark reality. They were given a great foundation, but the real building project never really got started.

The Apostle Paul understood this dilemma. He told the Corinthian believers that he couldn't give them solid food since they were still babies needing milk. This was a church that had all the spiritual gifts in operation; this was a church that we would say today was alive and full of the Spirit! But here Paul says they were still in spiritual nappies and so he couldn't give them the real meat of the gospel.

He was talking about the immorality in the church; strife among believers; marriage problems; food sacrificed to idols; insubordination; abuses of the Lord's Supper; spiritual gifts; the resurrection of the dead and how to take an offering. Nothing but milk, Paul said. However, he did give us a little peek at the solid food in 1 Corinthians 2:6-16. Then the next verse (3:1) goes back to addressing people as babes in Christ.

So, what is Paul talking about in chapter 2? He tells us in another place about his personal trip to the central offices of the universe where he *"heard inexpressible words, which a man is not permitted to speak."* Who knows what God shared with Paul then, He never included that in the New Testament. The Epistles, we must remember, are corrections. We don't have the mainstream of the Apostolic teaching - only the corrections. We don't have all that Paul taught when he was actually in Corinth, Antioch, Troas, Thessalonica and the other cities.

What is the book of Romans about? It is a basic, yet detailed outline of the gospel - man's need for a saviour and our abundance in Christ. What about Hebrews? Well, the writer himself, as we saw earlier, said that he had to water it down so as to not choke the spiritual babies.

Doesn't that disturb you a little to know that the Book of Romans and the book of Hebrews; the 'heavy' books of the New Testament; the books they leave until the third year in Theological College because they are so deep; doesn't it unsettle you to learn that they too are just spiritual milk?

So much of what we do and what is preached today is not designed to mature and perfect the body of Christ. God's mandate to those who lead and teach is clear. It is laid out for us by the Apostle Paul:

> **Ephesians 4:11-13** *"So Christ himself gave the apostles, the prophets, the evangelists, the pastors and teachers, to equip his people for works of service, so that the body of Christ may be built up until we all reach unity in the faith and in the knowledge of the Son of God and become mature, attaining to the whole measure of the fullness of Christ."*

My job is to equip the saints, to bring them to maturity. I was never taught that in church or in Bible College. I had been taught how to entertain people and how to attract people to my church, not how to perfect them.

The vast majority of the activities of the church across the world today, especially the mega churches, are designed to entertain, to maintain and to keep people involved.

We desperately need a rebirth of this apostolic ministry. The writer of Hebrews knew this frustration when he said, *"Though by this time you ought to be teachers, you have need again for someone to teach you the elementary principles."* (5:12). He was obviously expecting something better - that many of the laymen would eventually become teachers.

Ephesians 4 doesn't say that the apostles, prophets and pastors are to *do* the work of service. It says they are to equip the saints to do that. An architect does not build buildings; he plans how others should do it. If the architect had to follow through and lay all the bricks and construct the building - he may only get to build a few buildings in his whole career. As it is, however, he can effectively build several at once.

We need church leaders who can draw up God's blueprints and equip the believers to put the building together. This is discipleship. This is equipping people to truly follow Jesus.

The overall goal, Paul says, is to *"attain to the measure of the stature which belongs to the fullness of Christ."* God wants everyone to grow and minister just as Jesus did and that's why the Holy Spirit has come.

When Jesus said, "Follow me ..." He meant ALL the way.

He was (and is) saying to us all: *"Come with Me through all the ups and downs of life and ministry; learn from Me; laugh with Me; cry with Me; experience My broken heart over the lost; taste My suffering, My rejection, My death and come with Me as we rise triumphant again."*

It's not all bads news though. I sincerely believe the Lord has been slowly taking more and more of His people down this discipleship road. I believe there has been more real spiritual growth in some parts of the church over recent years than in many decades beforehand.

We are not really seeing it in swelling numbers and flashy demonstrations of power. We see it in our own suffering and struggles as we try to find God in the fog of unrealised expectations and disappointments. We see it in the growth and maturing of those believers who spend time in the valley, not striving to climb the mountain, but letting God do what He desires to do in them when things are not going well. All of my teaching over many years has been aimed at moving people from on from the elementary things - the diet of milk - and helping them to get their teeth into the meat of God's Word and the true depth of the gospel. I want us to know what it means to really follow Jesus - all the way and wherever He leads us. I want us to understand that we will never share His glory if we never share His pain.

My prayer is that we will commit to the discipleship journey seriously and press on to embrace what God has planned for us. I pray that we will have the courage to finally put away our bottles and bibs and get out our steak knives and ask the Lord to show us the way as we follow Him with total abandonment and faith as He leads us through the highs and lows of life in this broken world and shows us how to more fully embrace His Kingdom, for His glory.

2. THE INVITATION

As we move into this teaching series about following Jesus, let's go all the way back to the beginning as we are reminded of where this all began.

> **Matthew 4:18-22** *"As Jesus was walking beside the Sea of Galilee, he saw two brothers, Simon called Peter and his brother Andrew. They were casting a net into the lake, for they were fishermen. "Come, follow me," Jesus said, "and I will send you out to fish for people." At once they left their nets and followed him. Going on from there, he saw two other brothers, James son of Zebedee and his brother John. They were in a boat with their father Zebedee, preparing their nets. Jesus called them, and immediately they left the boat and their father and followed him."*

> **Luke 5:27-28** *"After this, Jesus went out and saw a tax collector by the name of Levi sitting at his tax booth. "Follow me," Jesus said to him, and Levi got up, left everything and followed him."*

What Jesus was really saying was simple, and yet incredibly confronting. He was saying, *"Follow me and I will make you fishers of men and women. Follow me and I will connect you with the power that created this universe. Follow me and I will take you on a journey into the supernatural realm - right into the middle of a cosmic battle between the powers of light and darkness."*

In the first chapter of this book, I began to explore what it means to really follow Jesus; what it means to get our teeth into the 'meat' of discipleship; to grow up spiritually and leave the 'milk' of elementary teachings behind us. We were challenged from the New Testament book of Hebrews to accept the possibility that we might be spiritual babies, still consuming the 'milk' of the kingdom of God.

By now many of us should be teachers and equippers of others and yet we may well still have a diet of milk. This confronting challenge comes as an encouragement to press on and mature in Christ. It does not come as a judgement to any of us. It's this 'meat' of discipleship that I want us to discover in this study and begin to chew on as we ask the question: *What does it really mean to follow Jesus?*

I decided to look up all the references in the Gospels where Jesus said, *"Follow me."* I found over twenty of them and it was really fascinating to notice the response of those to whom Jesus issued this invitation. They either dropped everything and walked with Him, with no thought to their own possessions or anything - or they just walked away from Him because the cost was too high. They are the only responses we can make to the call of Jesus. Let's read more of those passages:

> **Matthew 8:18-22** *"When Jesus saw the crowd around him, he gave orders to cross to the other side of the lake. Then a teacher of the law came to him and said, "Teacher, I will follow you wherever you go." Jesus replied, "Foxes have dens and birds have nests, but the Son of Man has no place to lay his head." Another disciple said to him, "Lord, first let me go and bury my father." But Jesus told him, "Follow me, and let the dead bury their own dead.""*

As a young person first reading that passage, I thought this was an incredibly heartless thing for Jesus to say to this man who had just lost his father. I am sure it appeared pretty cruel to the man. But I have since come to understand that Jesus was deliberately using such an emotive scenario in our human life to point out the priority of our spiritual walk and discipleship. Another person who was not willing to pay the price was the rich young man we encounter in this passage in Matthew:

Matthew 19:23-24 *"Then Jesus said to his disciples, "Truly I tell you, it is hard for someone who is rich to enter the kingdom of heaven. Again I tell you, it is easier for a camel to go through the eye of a needle than for someone who is rich to enter the kingdom of God."*

Now I'm sure we all know Jesus is not preaching against wealth or money here. He is also not saying that those who have financial security in this life will not enter the kingdom of heaven. He is talking about the attitude of our heart. If our heart attitude to anything is such that Jesus gets second place on our priority list, then we will not experience the glory and the fullness of the kingdom of God, for that only comes to a totally surrendered heart. Jesus looked into the rich man's heart and saw that his wealth was really the most important thing in his life - there was no room for Jesus.

If we are to follow Jesus, He must be our first priority; His mission must be our primary concern. That doesn't mean that we leave everything behind literally - at times that is what He calls some of us to do - but most often that is not practical. But He does call us to leave everything behind in our hearts as we put Him first in everything.

Now before we all jump in to affirm that Jesus is first in our hearts, let's be careful to evaluate our lives, our actions and our priorities - the things we think, say and do every day - before we affirm that Jesus is first. Because if Jesus truly is first, it will be very obvious to all around us. That story in Matthew 19 is very confronting and challenging. Jesus is actually saying that nothing should stand ahead of Him, His ministry and the Kingdom of God. He uses a very emotive example of our own families to make the point that we live in another realm, we are citizens of an eternal reality and it is in that eternal spiritual realm, that Kingdom, where our priorities must lie.

This physical human kingdom in which we now reside is but a drop in the ocean of eternity. The years that we reside on this planet are just a very brief stopover in our eternal existence. For we never die. Every human soul it eternal. We will all live forever, whether we believe in Jesus or not. We will either live in His presence under His love, or we will live outside His presence, but we will all live forever. So, Jesus is setting the scene for that eternity by saying that if we are to follow Him then He is to be No. 1. then He is to have our greatest loyalty, allegiance and our deepest love. This is what Jesus meant here:

Matthew 16:24 *"If anyone would come after Me, he must deny himself and take up his cross and follow me."*

There have been many sermons preached and many books written which try to explain what it might mean to deny ourselves. The truth is: this self-denial will be different for everyone. For some it will be very literal and all the way. Some will sell everything, own nothing and live totally by faith from day to day and serve Jesus in a full-time ministry capacity. That is their calling and conviction.

Others will have successful careers, a nice home, cars and material wealth, but choose to use that wealth for Jesus and His Kingdom. Their role is just as important and the fact that they have material wealth and possessions does not mean that they have not taken their discipleship seriously.

Of course, I need to stress that it is much, much harder for these people to really embrace the meat of discipleship, for their wealth and personal security will always try to lure them away from Jesus. That's why our Lord said that it is easier for a camel to go through the eye of a needle than for a rich man to enter the kingdom of heaven.

Again, He was talking about our heart attitude here. If we are possessive, protective or selfish in regard to our wealth, we will not taste the succulent steak of God's kingdom. We will always fall back on our man-made security.

In the kingdom of God, Jesus is the rock upon which we stand; He is our security; He is our focus; He is the One Who holds our life together. Financial security, possessions and wealth can often get in the way of us acknowledging the Lordship of Christ, but they don't have to.

It is certainly not impossible for us to follow Jesus and be surrounded by material wealth, but it is much harder. The pressures placed on us in an affluent society and in this 'enlightened' technological age are tremendous. It is much harder to be a true disciple in our culture today than at any point in history.

I believe that is one of the reasons why the vast majority of revivals that have broken out across the world and have continued over long periods of time have been in poorer parts of the world where people simply don't have much to give up as they follow Jesus.

When Jesus issues the invitation to deny themselves and follow Him, these people jump at the opportunity because they have very little to lose. When Jesus issues the same invitation in the rich, materialistic western world, there is a much stronger reluctance to make Jesus No.1, because in human terms we have so much more to lose.

I also believe it was easier for the first disciples to follow Jesus than it is for us. They really had no idea what they were letting themselves in for. When Jesus stood by the lake that day and called those guys to follow Him so He could make them 'fishers of men,' they just went.

They left everything they owned and everything that was important to them and followed Jesus. I am not wanting to minimise their obedience or sacrifice - there was a very real cost for them to follow Jesus. But had they known the real cost; had they known what was coming, perhaps their willingness to drop their nets and leave their jobs to follow Him would have been a little weaker.

They didn't know what we now know. They didn't know that when Jesus called them to follow Him - He called them to a whole life of self-denial. They had no idea where He was headed. They had no concept of Calvary. There wasn't even a hint which told them that after spending day and night with this very special Man, they would then watch the Romans torture Him to death on a cruel cross. They were not aware that they would be the laughingstock of the whole society, scorned and ridiculed because they followed a loser who promised the world and delivered nothing.

I would therefore suggest that it was easier for Peter, James and John and all the others to say 'yes' when Jesus issued that invitation than it is for you and me today. Because we now have the full picture. We have the whole of Church history to look back on. We have all of the Scriptures to read. We have the Holy Spirit resident within us to reveal the heart and purposes of God. We know more of the cost of true discipleship than those early brothers and sisters. When we say 'yes' to Jesus and follow Him, it takes a lot of courage and faith - or at least it should.

As I was reflecting on this over the past week or two, I began to wonder how superficial our commitment to follow Jesus really is. On the one hand, we should know the implications of discipleship because it is so clearly laid out in Scripture and Church history books. We know what real disciples of Jesus face in this life.

And yet I look around the Church today and I see millions of people who have said 'yes' to Jesus at some point, but they aren't really following Him. They are not really on that journey; they're not walking beside Him in His ministry. They have made some kind of commitment or decision or intellectual affirmation of faith which gives them the label of *Christian*, but they are not a true disciple yet.

They may be affirming Who Jesus is and what He has done for them, but they are not following Him, because to follow someone - you have to move! Jesus is going somewhere. Jesus is always on the move. The ministry He began when He was on earth, He continues today through His Spirit. So, when we say we are followers of Jesus, that's what we should be doing. You can't follow someone unless you go where they go. It sounds ridiculously simple, doesn't it? But we need it to be ridiculously simple sometimes so we can see the futility of what we are doing or not doing.

I want to suggest that there are millions of people in this world who call themselves disciples of Jesus; who say they are followers of Him; and yet they are not going anywhere in their spiritual walk. If they are true followers of Jesus, then Jesus hasn't done much in a long, long time! Do you get my point?

I want us to look at Jesus' invitation to follow Him in a fresh light, with a renewed focus on the implications of accepting that invitation. Jesus is calling us to follow Him in every moment of every day. He is always asking us to follow Him; never demanding; never ordering; but always inviting. We can ignore that invitation; we can accept it superficially and *think* we are following Him; or we can look at it honestly, count the cost of saying 'yes' and then pay the price of being a real disciple. For we all know how easy it is to follow Jesus when things are going our way.

We know how easy it is to follow Jesus when the party is on and things are really happening and it's obvious He's there. Anyone can follow Jesus when everything's going well. There were many in those early years who found it easy to follow Jesus when He was healing the sick. They found it easy to follow Jesus when He was raising the dead and turning water into wine at a wedding and healing a man's crippled hand. They found it easy to follow Jesus when He was on the Mount of transfiguration. They found it easy to follow Jesus when He was preaching with such authority and slamming the religious leaders who had oppressed the people for so long. They found it easy to follow Jesus when They found it easy to follow Jesus on Palm Sunday as they cried out *'hosanna to the Son of David.'* When the majority of people around you are crying out His name, it's very easy to say: *"I'm His friend … I know Him … I'm on His team … I'm a true disciple."*

But as those disciples soon learned, there is a flipside to following Jesus. It's not a party every day and when Jesus' call to follow Him led them to the last supper, there was confusion; there was pain; there was betrayal. When His call to follow Him led them into the garden of Gethsemane, all they could do was sleep. When His call to follow Him reached a climax on Calvary's hill, it was all too much and very few willing followers stood with Him at the end.

Where were the hundreds and thousands of worshippers from the previous week when their king finally did what He came to do? Where were the crowds that pushed around Him for three long years as He ministered with power and authority? Where were the hundreds of people who had been healed and restored to life because of this Man; people whose whole lives had been changed by one touch or one word from this Man; where were they when Jesus was writhing in agony on the cross?

Is it too harsh to say that the only genuine disciples; the only committed followers of Jesus; were those few at the foot of the cross? All the others only followed Him while He was going where they thought He should go. To them, Jesus took a dreadfully wrong turn in that final week and got Himself arrested and killed. At that point, Jesus started to discover who His real followers were.

The hard truth is this: either we follow Him all the way, or we don't follow Him at all. We stand with Him at the foot of that cross and participate in His death and we share in His suffering, or we are not a true disciple. We find it easy to follow Jesus into a church that it alive and vibrant and has all the external signs of being healthy and alive.

We find it easy to follow Jesus when the worship is anointed and we have great music. We find it easy to follow Jesus when our Church is growing numerically and everyone's smiling and happy. We find it easy to follow Jesus when we see His Spirit at work in power.

We find it easy to follow Jesus when we understand what it is He's calling us to do and why. We find it easy to follow Jesus when He does what we think He's going to do or when the outcome is predictable or what we prayed for comes about. We find it easy to follow Jesus when there is a clear explanation as to why something went wrong.

We find it easy to follow Jesus when those around us are following Jesus. We find it easy to follow Jesus when there's money in the bank and food on the table and the children are healthy and the job is going well and our life is working. But where are we when things don't go our way? How easy is it to follow Jesus when the answer to our prayer is not what we expected? How easy is it to follow Jesus when we are part of a church that is not growing numerically?

How easy is it to follow Jesus when the worship doesn't suit our tastes? How easy is it to follow Jesus when there are people in the church to whom we can't relate and prefer not to even be around? How easy is it to follow Jesus when the tide of public opinion turns against us in some way?

How easy is it to follow Jesus when those close to us in the church turn on us and become critical and even betray us? How easy is it to follow Jesus when He goes into the heart of our city late at night and hangs around the drunks and the homeless and the criminals and the prostitutes and the drug dealers? How easy is it to follow Jesus when we discern that an overseas country needs us more than our country does - when the call to a distant mission field comes and our whole life is turned upside down?

Jesus is everywhere - often in the most unlikely places - but His saving, healing, redeeming ministry continues and He challenges us to find Him in those places and join Him there. So many times, we move off in a direction and say that we are following Jesus, but He's not going that way and we don't want to admit it.

Throughout this study, I want us to re-evaluate our current direction in life. Are we following Jesus or are we following a man or a woman or a denomination or a concept? Are we following Jesus or are following our own pre-determined plans and goals which did not come from Him. Look at the road you are on right now in your life and ask yourself, is Jesus here? Is this the road He is on? Is this where the action is? Is this His ministry? Am I truly following Him? Is He my highest priority? Does He have my deepest loyalty? Is He the recipient of my greatest love? Is He the One to Whom I ultimately submit all? He is the author of my faith but is He finisher of it also? He got me into this race, but am I now running it without Him?

Is He the One to Whom I yield every moment of every day? In my life, is He the Alpha and the Omega, the beginning and the end, the first and the last?

Or is Jesus just one of the many components of my life. He is in their somewhere as one of many things that occupy my time. I have family, I have work, I have various interests, I have hobbies, I have pleasures … and I have Jesus. Is that the way it is? Be honest. Is He part of your life? Or is He your life? I challenge you to look up all the references where Jesus said: *"Follow Me"* and try to get a picture of what it means to follow Jesus.

He is out there right now in your community getting His hands dirty in thousands of people's lives. Marriage disputes; domestic violence; crime; drugs; immorality - He's in the middle of the whole mess with His sleeves rolled up, loving people back to life. Where are we? When He says *"Follow Me"* is that where we want to go? Is that where we will commit to go?

Or will we be selective in how we follow Jesus:

"Oh yes, I'll follow you here to worship each week … that doesn't cost me much … or hurt much … but out there … I'm not so sure. I have nothing to offer those people. I am not qualified to meet their needs."

Well, I recall that over 2,000 years ago, Jesus gathered a small band of roughnecks together who really didn't seem qualified for anything special either and they turned the world upside down and inside out. None of them had the ability to do that - Jesus did it - they were just available to be used by Him in that process. He is not interested in your ability it is your *availability* that He is looking for.

Jesus never told us to go somewhere and do something without Him. There is this embedded concept in our minds that Jesus *sends* us to do things. We use the terminology all the time of Jesus sending us. The translators even used it in the Bible. But when someone sends you, you go away from them to the place they sent you. When Jesus sends you, He never leaves you. That's why we need to use a different word. Jesus doesn't *send* us … Jesus *calls* us. Jesus is already there. He is already doing the stuff and He invites us to join Him in His ministry.

Jesus doesn't send a person to Africa as a missionary. From the heart of Africa, Jesus calls that person to join Him there as co-labourers. Jesus doesn't send us into the heart of our community to minister to the needs of people; He is already there - ministering day and night. Jesus simply issues the invitation to follow Him there so we can participate in His ministry. It is always <u>His</u> ministry. It is in <u>His</u> power, by <u>His</u> strength and <u>His</u> authority that all this happens.

In fact, I would suggest that everything Jesus calls us to do, we simply cannot do. Every command, every exhortation to holiness and service and godliness and good works we read in the Bible - we simply can't do it. It is by the Lord's power and in the Lord's strength and by His authority that anything at all happens in this world and that is particularly true of Christian ministry. So, when Jesus calls us to follow Him, that's what we are to do, we are to follow Him and participate in what He is already doing.

When we look with human eyes alone, the task of being a disciple is a daunting one indeed. Some days the needs of the world overwhelm us as we look in the mirror and say, 'What on earth am I doing here?' That is not the time to look in the mirror - it's the time to look at Jesus. To fix your eyes upon Him and Him only. For His bidding is His enabling.

The One Who calls you to follow Him is the also the One Who empowers you to follow Him. All He wants from you and me is the willingness to go. He wants a heart attitude of genuine submission, surrender and obedience. He doesn't want anything else from us, for we have nothing else to offer! We can give Him absolutely nothing that will add to His ministry; we can achieve nothing for His glory; without His strength, His power and His enabling presence. Our task is to say *"Yes!"* when we hear Jesus say, *"Follow me."*

The invitation from Jesus is issued right now afresh to you and to me, to take up our cross, deny ourselves and to follow Him. Let's pray that He will give us the courage and ability to accept that invitation with a fresh commitment today, knowing that it is always in His strength and by His authority and power that we even live and breathe!

3. THE SUBMISSION TEST

So far in this study, we have been challenged to consider the implications of Jesus' invitation to follow Him. As we have seen in some of the gospel accounts, many people who were confronted with Jesus' offer to follow Him - turned away because the cost was too great. They wanted to maintain control of their lives; they did not want to surrender or submit to Him; they wanted to be masters of their own destiny, rather than trust everything to Him.

However, we have also seen that those who did respond positively to Jesus' invitation, went all the way. Many of them literally left everything that was important to them in this world and followed Him without hesitation. This total, unreserved submission and commitment to Jesus was, and still is, the hallmark of true discipleship.

Once we have said 'yes' to Jesus, the discipleship road is winding and at times very narrow. It can have some major potholes and obstacles, but all the time we are assured of our Master's presence - leading us, guiding us, supporting us and at times even carrying us.

Along that discipleship road there are many tests. From the New Testament and Church history, we learn that every person who decided to follow Jesus with commitment and conviction, went through a period of training and refining.

In many ways that process continues throughout our whole life, but in our early days as a disciple, God's Spirit will lead us through many battles and tests. Not just to prove our loyalty, devotion and commitment to Him, but to also rid us of any self-reliance and idolatry.

As we study these discipleship tests in the remainder of this book, we will invariably be reminded of experiences we have had in our own Christian journey which we may not have seen as tests. In fact, we may not have seen the hand of God in any of those circumstances.

It is my prayer that we will look at all that happens in our life - the joys and the pain - as tools in the hand of God as He refines us, purifies us and removes our self-focus and self-reliance more and more so that the true character of Jesus that lies within each of us as believers can fully emerge.

The first test on the discipleship road is one that will never leave us in this life - it will always be there. This is a test that we must continually face if we are to push on to the 'meat' and embrace God's abundant life for each of us. This is the submission test - one of the hardest tests of all at times - but one we must embrace to grow and mature. The writer of Hebrews gives us an amazing insight into the life of Jesus:

> **Hebrews 5:7-9** *"During the days of Jesus' life on earth, he offered up prayers and petitions with fervent cries and tears to the one who could save him from death, and he was heard because of his reverent submission. Son though he was, he learned obedience from what he suffered and, once made perfect, he became the source of eternal salvation for all who obey him."*

Jesus was heard because of His reverent submission. He was a Son, but learned obedience from what He suffered. This is Jesus we are talking about - the Son of God - the King of Kings - the Lord of Lords, and yet as a human being; a man with the same limitations as you and me; He learned obedience from what He suffered. He was heard because of His reverent submission to the Father.

Even Jesus knew the potholes and the dangers on that road. In fact, He showed us the way. He came and took upon our flesh and walked that road before the Father. He not only secured our salvation because of His atoning death and glorious resurrection; He showed us the way.

He felt our pain; He experienced our frustrations; He confronted our temptations; He lived in our world and related to the Father the way we have to.

Jesus walked our discipleship road, paving the way for each of us. More than any other human being, Jesus Christ passed the submission test.

> **Philippians 2:5-8** *"In your relationships with one another, have the same mindset as Christ Jesus: Who, being in very nature God, did not consider equality with God something to be used to his own advantage; rather, he made himself nothing by taking the very nature of a servant, being made in human likeness. And being found in appearance as a man, he humbled himself by becoming obedient to death - even death on a cross!"*

The example of submission that Jesus has given us all is incredibly powerful. We are talking about God incarnate; the Creator and Sustainer of the universe in human flesh; the greatest authority in all of creation; yet look at His incredible submission in the first thirty years of His life. He grew up as a little boy, submitting to human parents. He submitted to their parental authority, even though He held all authority.

He submitted to human teachers and trainers, even though He was the source of all knowledge, truth and wisdom. The Creator was sitting under the tutoring of His creatures! How incredible is that?

He learned a trade; worked with His hands; made things out of wood - things which, to the humans around Him must have seemed beautifully and skilfully made. But these same hands made the very trees from which the wood came; these hands flung the stars and galaxies into space; and yet these hands also submitted to the primitive ways of man.

What an example of submission we have in Jesus! He did not exert His authority. He did not over-step the mark. He did not even commence His ministry until the Father said the time was right, which was the day of His baptism when the Holy Spirit descended upon Him like a dove and anointed Him for the unique ministry for which He came.

We have so much teaching about those last three years of His life; we focus so much on those years and that is understandable, but what about the first thirty years? I believe Jesus' life speaks to us just as powerfully in those early years as it does in the final three years. He lived a life of humble, obedient submission to God and to others.

That submission continued right through His ministry years. Day and night, He continued being in submission to the Father - withdrawing sometimes for whole nights of prayer. This is the Son of the living God, but He set aside His divine privileges and became subject to the same limitations as you and me. He spent hours and hours crying out to the Father and He was heard because of His reverent submission.

There were so many times in His life and ministry where He could have called the shots. He was the man on the scene; He could have made all the decisions; those around Him thought He did; but the Bible tells us that this was not the case.

John 5:19 *"Very truly I tell you, the Son can do nothing by himself; he can do only what he sees his Father doing, because whatever the Father does the Son also does."*

Jesus was in constant submission to the Father. Another time in Luke 5 we find Jesus teaching the crowd and the Father appeared to interrupt His Son so that someone could be healed. The text says that Jesus was teaching, and *"the power of God was present to heal"* - so Jesus stopped teaching in order to participate in what the Father was doing.

Let's not miss this powerful truth: Jesus; the Son of God; our ultimate example; the author and finisher of our faith; Jesus, stopped what He was doing so He could participate in what the Father was doing. Jesus was constantly in submission to the Father.

There is no doubt that Jesus is the ultimate example of someone who passed this submission test. But we have a Bible full of examples. Abraham, Noah, Moses, Job, David, the first disciples and Mary, the mother of Jesus - to mention just a few. There are many examples of those who faced this test of submission and passed. There are many others who, like King Saul, and many of the kings of Israel, faced the same test and failed miserably.

So, what about you and me? Each one of us has to face this same submission test every day if we are to travel this discipleship road. We have a daily choice to submit to God and trust Him and obey Him regardless of our own whims, desires and convictions; regardless of the opinions of those around us in the church and in the world.

Will we submit to the God of Abraham, Moses and David? Will we submit to the Father of our Lord Jesus Christ, the way Jesus did? Will we submit to each other?

Ephesians 5:21 says *"Submit to each other out of reference for Christ."* We are also called to submit to authorities in the church and the God-ordained authorities in our land. This theme of submission permeates the whole New Testament, but how does this manifest itself in our lives each day?

There are a number of examples. Mutual submission in a marriage; submission in our workplaces to authorities that may make decisions we don't agree with or understand - decisions which may not cause us to compromise our Christian convictions, but decisions which nonetheless we don't like and don't want to submit to. How do we face the submission test then? Do we submit to those authorities, as unto Christ?

What about our submission to the laws of the land? You may be thinking you are not a criminal ... why even ask such a question? Well, let me ask a different question: when was the last time you broke the speed limit wilfully and with little concern? What about the details on your tax return that could have been a little more accurate?

How are we going with submission in the church? How do we submit to leadership we don't agree with? The Bible tells us how ... we simply make the choice to submit. If the issue is that important to us - then we can confront the leadership and talk it through or we can place ourselves under a different leadership ... but remaining part of a body and choosing to not be in submission to the leaders of that body is sin and rebellion and it gives Satan a wonderful foothold to wreak havoc in the lives of many.

Sadly, because of false teaching and a concept of leadership that does not come from the Bible, we have inadvertently led thousands of Christians down a path that will bring them face to face with this test of submission.

This problem has been exacerbated because of a growing number of abusive leaders in the Church which can cause people to run the other way and never trust or submit to any leaders.

As we are reminded in the life of David, submission to a leader that we believe is doing the wrong thing is hard and trusting God to deal with that leader and raise up someone else in His time and His way is even harder - but that is the choice we must make daily if we are to pass this test of submission in the church.

It is really hard to serve under another person's vision; it is really hard to submit to a course of action or a direction that you are not in favour of personally; it isn't sinful, it's just not what you think should happen. But I have found that those who struggle with such submission will be tested over and over again. I have seen this reality in the church for years. God continues to place people who can't submit in churches with leaders who get up their nose and do it all wrong, in their humble opinion.

Some people refuse to confront their own sin of rebellion and pride so they run to another church fellowship, only to find that they can't submit to those leaders either, perhaps for different reasons! They are avoiding the submission test; not facing it with courage and determination.

There are people in the body of Christ who have never submitted to any leadership for any length of time and yet when you talk to them, they make it sound like they are the spiritual ones; the ones with discernment; the ones who can sniff out a bad leader from a hundred metres. That's why people like this usually end up running their own church or not being involved at all.

Now let me jump to the other side and say I know how hard it is to be in a church where your gifts, abilities or opinions don't seem to matter to the leadership. There are thousands of Christians in church all over the world who are not treated well by leaders and are ignored and not appreciated. That can be really tough. There are even those who, like David, are abused and criticised and hunted and attacked in some way by the existing leadership.

That is sad, and I wish it wasn't that way. I wish all leaders were perfect and could read the minds of all the people they lead. I wish God had set it up so that there could be no more crazy King Sauls. It would be so good if leaders always got it right and always heard from God at the right time. I wish a lot of things were different, but the fact remains that what we have is what God has given us and He calls each of us to trust Him more than any human authority and allow Him to do as He wishes with the leaders He chooses - whether we agree with them or like them or not.

Of course, our ultimate test of submission lies within our relationship with God. If we truly trust Jesus to build His church; if we let go the death grip we have on our ministries and our lives; if we humble ourselves before God; He will vindicate us in time. Abusive leaders will be dealt with in God's way, in His time. Perhaps it will be the attitude of our heart towards the leaders that will be dealt with. Either way, the church belongs to Jesus, not us. He was running it without our help or opinion long before we were born and He will continue to do so long after we have gone.

If you ever find yourself in such a situation; if you feel that who you are and what you have to offer is being overlooked by the leadership; then understand the test that God is placing before you - the submission test.

The real test of submission comes when you find yourself at odds with those to whom you are called to submit. If your gifts or conviction about a course of action or your desire to minister in a certain area is from God; if it is truly God Who has placed that in your heart; if your desire to exercise those gifts and fulfil that ministry to glorify and serve God is greater than your desire to be recognised or noticed or appreciated by others, then be patient - your day will come and God will open the door for you.

If you just want to feel important, be noticed or appreciated more, or do something that is more up-front, then that is just pride, it's ugly and evil, but very common. Just call it what it is, confess it and get over it. Be patient, be humble, and trust God to open the doors for you if and when He chooses.

Until then, join Jesus in His life of reverent submission. You may have to serve under someone else's vision; you may have to submit to someone you don't agree with for years before God raises you up - but the call to submission will never disappear. You can complain to God about that; you can kick and scream and cry 'unfair'; you can refuse to submit; it's your choice. Just don't expect to travel much further down the discipleship road until you have firmly embraced the submission test.

Ultimately our submission is to God, but often He will test our trust and faith and submission to Him by calling us to submit to others.

4. THE OBEDIENCE TEST

In this chapter I want us to look at another test which faces us on the discipleship road: the obedience test. This is the test that Adam and Eve failed back in the very beginning. God decreed how they should live and what they should do and not do if they were to experience the abundance of life in paradise. They failed this test and the consequences flowed down through all of God's creation.

The 'second Adam', Jesus, also faced this obedience test many times. In fact, it was the first real test He faced at the commencement of His ministry. It was almost as though it was an initiation or probationary test of some kind before He commenced His three-year teaching ministry.

You will recall that John the Baptist preached about the coming Messiah and prepared the way for Jesus and His ministry. Then on that special day in the Jordan river, Jesus was baptised and the Father gave His approval and blessing to His Son. The Holy Spirit descended upon Him and anointed Him for the ministry ahead. Now it is fascinating to see where the Spirit led Jesus immediately after that:

> **Luke 4:1-13** *"Jesus, full of the Holy Spirit, left the Jordan and was led by the Spirit into the wilderness, where for forty days he was tempted by the devil. He ate nothing during those days, and at the end of them he was hungry. The devil said to him, "If you are the Son of God, tell this stone to become bread." Jesus answered, "It is written: 'Man shall not live on bread alone.'" The devil led him up to a high place and showed him in an instant all the kingdoms of the world. And he said to him, "I will give you all their authority and splendour; it has been given to me, and I can give it to anyone I want to.*

If you worship me, it will all be yours." Jesus answered, "It is written: 'Worship the Lord your God and serve him only.'"

The devil led him to Jerusalem and had him stand on the highest point of the temple. "If you are the Son of God," he said, "throw yourself down from here. For it is written: 'He will command his angels concerning you to guard you carefully; they will lift you up in their hands, so that you will not strike your foot against a stone.'"

Jesus answered, "It is said: 'Do not put the Lord your God to the test.'" When the devil had finished all this tempting, he left him until an opportune time.

With the Father's approval at His baptism, it is now time for Jesus to begin His earthly campaign. But before we begin a campaign, we must choose our methods. The story of Jesus' temptation shows us how He chooses once and for all the method by which He proposes to win the lost to God. It shows us how Jesus rejects the way of power and glory and embraces the way of suffering and the cross.

Jesus knew why He had come. He knew He had come to die. He knew He had come to be Isaiah's suffering servant. He knew that His calling was to walk the road of suffering and death. So here, at the very commencement of Jesus' earthly ministry, God uses His own archenemy, Satan, to test Jesus' obedience to that call. Let me just paint the picture behind this story for you.

This occurred in the wilderness. The inhabited part of Judea stood on the central plateau which was the backbone of southern Palestine. Between it and the Dead Sea stretched a terrible wilderness. It was 35 miles long and 15 miles wide. It was called *Jeshimmon*: which means *"the devastation."*

The hills were like dust heaps. The limestone looked blistering and peeling. The rocks were bare and jagged. The ground sounded hollow to the horses' hooves. It glowed with heat like a vast furnace and it ran out to the precipices - 1200 feet high - which swooped down to the Dead Sea. It was there in that devastation that Jesus found Himself alone, confronted by the full force of evil.

These temptations didn't just come one after the other like scenes in a play. We need to think of Jesus being led to this lonely place by the Holy Spirit, and for forty long days He wrestled with this whole problem of how He would win people for the Father. It was a battle that never really ended until the cross and the empty tomb. That's why the last line in this story says that Satan left Jesus, but only for a while.

The first temptation was to turn stones into bread. You may be aware that the wilderness was not just sand. It was covered with little limestone rocks shaped like loaves of bread. So, when you've gone without food that long and you possess the power that created the whole universe, then the temptation is strong. So, Satan effectively says to Jesus: *"If you want people to follow you, use your powers to give them material things."* The Tempter was suggesting that Jesus could bribe people with material things. Jesus answered with a quote from Deuteronomy 8:3 and declared that God's people will never find life in material things.

The task of Christianity is not to produce new conditions, the real task is to produce new people. The whole message of Christianity and the ministry of all true disciples is to see hearts turned back to God - the rest us up to God. Our task is to turn hearts to God, not tempt them with material things; not temp them with a prosperity doctrine that does not come from God; not tempt them by promising that life will be easy and things will always go their way.

Man does not live by bread alone. There is an eternal reality that is far deeper and far more significant than this life here on earth. That's why Jesus said later in His ministry: "*Seek first the kingdom of God and all these things will be added unto you.*" Seek first those things which are eternal, and those things which are temporal will follow.

In the second temptation, Jesus (in His imagination) stood on a mountain from which He could see the whole civilised world. This is the temptation to compromise. Satan called Jesus to compromise just a little, and people would follow Him. Jesus retorted and affirmed that God is God, right is right and wrong is wrong. There can be no compromise in the war with evil. Jesus quotes Deuteronomy 6 to thwart Satan's second attempt to lead Him astray.

It is a constant temptation to seek to win people by striking a compromise with the devil or the evil world around us. It is so easy for the church and for individual Christians to mix a little bit of the world into their discipleship to make it more palatable. We then end up with no black and white issues anymore; everything is relative; everything is grey; everything is acceptable; nothing can really be challenged.

Once again, Jesus is our key example here. He was loving, compassionate, kind, gracious, humble, always giving - rarely receiving. He was gentle and meek and but His standards were absolute. His judgements were precise. He used the Scriptures and articulated God's uncompromising view of sin, Satan, the world and Christian ministry.

On the discipleship road, you and I will be faced with decisions like this every day. Will we take the easy road and water-down the truth of who God is and who we are in Christ? Or will we stand firm like Jesus?

I am not talking about standing on our high moral ground and preaching against immorality and perversions in the community. Jesus didn't waste much time talking about such things. I am talking about the absolutes in the kingdom God: Who God is; who we are in Christ; who Satan is and what the mission of Jesus Christ is all about. The moral issues are of secondary importance, I believe. Invariably, such issues disappear or are dealt with when foundational issues are addressed.

One of the more serious errors in church life is not the watering down of moral issues, as serious as that may be - I think the greater sin in my opinion is that we water down the truth of what it means to be a real disciple. We water down or ignore passages about suffering, self-denial, death, spiritual warfare and the reality of demonic attacks against obedient servants of God. We water down or ignore issues like Church discipline, submission, working together as a team. In so many areas of church life we are tempted to compromise the truth of God's word and make life easier for ourselves. We don't want to tread on people's toes, so we let things that are wrong continue unchecked.

Pastors and their families are being destroyed every day in by those churches who have lost the plot when it comes to authority, obedience, submission and love. There are also many people in churches who are victims of abusive leaders who have lost the plot also. There is a spirit of rebellion in this nation that goes right back to our roots as a convict colony. The 'tall poppy syndrome' is as widespread and as ugly and as ever. There is also an anti-authoritarian attitude that is built into the very fabric of our society. If Christians don't identify that, confess it, own it, and ask the Lord to remove it, then it creeps into the church and when that rebellion manifests fully in the church, it is devastating.

If we are to walk together on this discipleship road, we must stand against the temptations of the enemy to conform to the patterns of this world. Submission, servanthood and self-sacrificial obedience are not common characteristics in the world around us today, they are as rare as diamonds and just as precious. Yet if we are to believe the Bible, such character traits are to be the norm in the kingdom of God. As we journey together as disciples, we need to stand against these temptations, pray for each other, support each other, be honest and confess these sins as they manifest in us and let God renew our minds and hearts.

In the third temptation, Jesus finds Himself on the pinnacle of the temple where Solomon's porch and the royal porch meet. There was a sheer drop of 450 feet down to the Kidron Valley below. This temptation faces us in the church every day. It's the temptation to give people a show. Jesus said, *"No, you must not use the power of God for such senseless demonstrations."* He was again quoting Scripture, referring to Deuteronomy 6:16.

Jesus saw quite clearly that if He used His power in this sensational way, He could just be a nine-day-wonder. The sensationalists never last. It is the hard road of service and suffering that leads to the cross that Jesus takes and calls us to take with Him - there is no other way. The crown comes after the cross, there are no shortcuts.

The modern church with all its experience, technology and ability to impress, is facing this third temptation every day. The temptation to put on a good show. We have the ability to impress people. We can get the best musicians and the finest music and the most creative order of service and we can put on a show that will impress even the most apathetic of audiences. We can do it with sincerity and conviction.

We can even cover it with prayer and truly believe that we are preaching the Gospel. Now, there is nothing wrong with any of that. But is that the method we should be adopting on a daily basis as we work out our salvation and live as disciples of the King?

If we look at the life of Jesus, we see very clearly that there was no sensationalism. His miracles were truly sensational - there is no doubt about it - but that was not His reason for healing people, raising them from the dead and delivering them from demonic oppression. It was His compassion for people in bondage that motivated Him to perform such miracles. He used the timing of those miracles to prove a point to the Pharisees and to build people's faith, but He never just put on a show.

Like Jesus, we have a choice to obey the call of God to be love-driven servants of all. We can choose to let compassion and love and other people's deepest needs drive us and direct us, or we can let our need to be noticed, successful or impressive in man's eyes, govern and motivate us. The road that the Father chose for His own Son was one of suffering, self-denial and death. It was a road of obedience.

In that obedience, Jesus was called to set aside His own power and glory and His personal interests and become like those around Him in order to win them for God. When He calls us to follow Him - we must do the same. If we are to obey the call of God, we must set aside our needs and our interests and our personal preferences and allow God's desires and plans and purposes to dominate all that we think say and do.

Jesus faced this test of obedience for forty long days in the wilderness, and He passed. He returned tired, hungry and broken, but He was totally surrendered to the will of God.

This wilderness experience for Jesus was not the only time He faced the obedience test. He faced it every single day as He made a deliberate choice to say 'yes' to God and 'no' to His flesh and 'no' to the world and 'no' to Satan. We live in a world where everyone is demanding their rights. Satan was very clever in the way He tempted Jesus. He reminded Him of who He was and the rights and privileges of such a position:

"If you are the Son of God (and Satan knew He was) then surely, it's the right of God's son to have the provision of food. He has the power to make food - let Him do it. Surely, it's the right of the Son of God to receive power over all nations and become King of Kings ... and since the world is in my hands ... I give it to you ... you only have to proclaim me as Lord. Surely, it's the right of the Son of God to claim protection against all dangers and His Father has actually promised it. So, let's put that promise to the test."

Jesus turns to Scripture each time and makes the point that He will obey God above everything else. He effectively says to Satan:

"You suggest that feeding my body should take precedence over obeying my Father? My God has told me that men, mere men, shall not live by bread alone .. therefore, nor shall I. You offer me universal power at the price of worshipping you .. but my Father has told men that they should worship nobody but Him ... therefore I shall not worship you. You propose that I should test my Father's promise of providential care to suit my own convenience ... but He has told men not to test Him in this way, therefore, neither shall I."

What is Jesus doing here? He is deliberately emptying Himself of His power and His glory. Jesus is deliberately forgoing His rights.

Satan was correct, as the Son of God, Jesus could do all those things. But He chose to put himself in the position of a man, under the authority of the law of God and walk in obedience to His Father.

This temptation scene has a familiar look. This scene played out many years earlier in the garden of Eden when the first Adam was given the same opportunity to obey or not. That Adam failed that test and set the whole human race on a course of destruction. Now the second Adam, Jesus Christ, alone in the wilderness, confronts the same tempter; faces the very same obedience test; and passes this test and puts mankind back on the right side of God and His purposes.

Jesus overcame the powers of hell by standing firm in His uncompromising obedience to the Word and will of the Father - an obedience that He pursued right through to the cross. This conflict in the wilderness was the very first time where a son of Adam raised an effective defence against Satan. The test of obedience is a hard test, it comes at times when we don't expect it or appreciate it, but it is a test we will continue to face on this discipleship road.

Many years ago, Keith Green took a verse out of the Old Testament and wrote a very powerful song around it. The opening line was, "*To obey is better than sacrifice.*" A constant theme of the Old Testament was obedience. God continued to tell His people that their sacrifices were a stench in His holy nostrils for they offered them with disobedient hearts. They made sacrifices to appease Him rather than obey Him to please Him. Sacrifices are fine, and God can really bless us for making those sacrifices, but if they are not the by-product of our obedience, then they are a waste of time. You can go out there and sell everything you own and give all the money to the church and commit your whole life to God in full-time service and not impress Him at all.

If that sacrifice was not in obedience to His call, to His Word; if God did not ask you to do that - then it was a total waste. We may make lots of sacrifices for God; we may give hundreds and hundreds of hours of our time to His service and work in His church; but if there are still things that we refuse to do that He asks of us, then all our sacrifices mean nothing.

You and I face this obedience test every day. Not just our obedience to the clear revelation of God's Word in the Bible - His *logos* - but obedience to that still small voice in our spirit - His *rhema* - His word to us personally. When that conviction comes, we have a choice to obey or rebel.

There are many who get stuck in this area and never travel any further on the discipleship road. If there is something that we are stubbornly refusing to let go of; to give up; to do or stop doing; if there is something that is not honouring to God that we continue to submit to; if there is a direction or course of action that He has showed us that we refuse to take; then we will come to a grinding halt on that road like a car with a broken axle.

Yes, it's true, our sin has been atoned for. Yes, it's true, God will not hold our sin against us as new covenant believers. But it is also true that our sin is still very real and it will continue to bring its consequences in this life. There is a consequence of disobedience. It's not the punishment of God - that all fell on Jesus. When we continue in sin, we invite Satan to manifest his presence and power in that sin and this will have serious consequences our lives and the lives of those around us. As we see in Jesus' temptations in the wilderness, when we stand against Satan in obedience to God, He departs from us - every time! Satan will flee when we resist Him - the Bible promises that and our experience confirms it.

So, what is God calling you to do or to be today? What does the obedience test mean for you right now? What choices are you this week? Is there some area of sin in your life that continues to haunt you and drag you down? Is there some addiction or habit you can't seem break that continues to put you at odds with God's will? Have you been caught on a side road and can't get back to the main road in God's kingdom? Is there something that God has called you to do and you just can't find the emotional energy or motivation or courage to pursue it?

Is the price too high? Is the cost too great? Is the sacrifice too painful? What is Jesus calling you to do? If you don't know, then you need to spend some time with Him seeking His direction and will for your life.

May the Spirit of God help us to face the obedience test each day with courage, with determination and with the power of God within us, making it possible to always submit to His will.

5. THE SERVANT TEST

What does it really mean to be a disciple of Jesus Christ? What does it really mean on a day-to-day basis to follow Him and be yielded to Him and walk the path He walked and is walking? As distinct from the superficial allegiance that we may give Jesus, I have been attempting in this book to help readers digest the 'meat' of discipleship, the nitty gritty of truly following Jesus.

As we have already seen, when Jesus issued the invitation for people to follow Him - some gave up everything and followed Him wholeheartedly while others counted the cost, shook their head and walked away. For those of us who do pursue this discipleship road, we are faced with many tests and we've explored some of those already here.

The first test we explored was the submission test. That is the test which we all face every day in our walk with Jesus. We are not only called to submit to Him and to His will, His Word and the prompting of His Spirit, we are called to submit to each other out of reverence for Christ. That whole area of submission is one that challenges us greatly in our anti-authoritarian culture.

The obedience test was the next one we encountered on the discipleship road. This is a test that Jesus was led by the Spirit to face in the wilderness at the very commencement of His ministry. Satan came against Him with great power and tempted Him to disobey the Father just the way he had with Adam in the Garden of Eden so long ago. The first Adam failed that test and sinned. The 'Second Adam' (Jesus) passed the test. For the first time ever, a man stood against the powers of darkness and remained obedient, thereby opening the way for each of us to do the same.

The next test that we face on the discipleship road is the servant test. I could write a whole book on servanthood, but I just want to touch on it here so we might understand how important it is if we are to truly follow Jesus. I will unpack this even more in the next chapter.

Jesus Christ is the ultimate servant. He was referred to way back in Isaiah 53 as *'The Suffering Servant'* - the One Who came not to be served but to serve; the One Who took the hand basin and towel and washed the feet of His disciples and calls us to do the same.

In Philippians 2 we read where Jesus made a choice to become a servant. He was equal with God, yet He chose to become a servant and became obedient unto death. In that same passage we are exhorted to have the same attitude and servant-heart as Jesus.

This theme of servanthood runs right through the New Testament. There are literally hundreds of verses referring to our mutual care and service of each other and our service to God in worship. As servants we are called to constantly yield our own desires and rights in order to serve the needs of others. This servant test is one that you and I face every day, and sadly we fail this test many times too.

Unfortunately, in our society, the term *servant* can trigger negative connotations. Some people think back to an African slave named *Kunte Kinte* and the Epic film *Roots.* Or the thousands of suppressed, underpaid people scrubbing floors and waiting on tables for the high and mighty of society.

The concept of a servant for many conjures up images of ignorance, objects of mistreatment, gross absence of human dignity and the epitome of many of the things that the Christian message opposes.

Many have the image of a servant as a pathetic creature with little or no will or purpose in life; bent over; crushed in spirit; lacking self-esteem; dirty, wrinkled and weary. But when we turn to the New Testament, we have a different picture. None of these descriptions come close to describing Jesus and yet He's the ultimate example of a servant.

In Matthew 23:11, Jesus said, " … *the greatest among you will be your servant."* He also said that the first will be the last and the servant of all. That's why even the Son of man came not as a mighty king on a throne in a castle surrounded by an army of thousands, but as a lowly, humble, suffering servant. It is God's desire that we do the same. Remember that grand declaration of assurance from Paul:

> **Romans 8:28-29** *"And we know that in all things God works for the good of those who love him, who have been called according to his purpose. For those God foreknew he also predestined to be conformed to the image of his Son, that he might be the firstborn among many brothers and sisters."*

Maybe you have never stopped to consider that God is committed to one major objective in the lives of all of His people and that is to conform us to the image of His Son. We are called to be servants. We are made to be like Jesus. Jesus declared His primary reason for being here:

> **Mark 10:45** *"Even the Son of Man did not come to be served, but to serve and to give His life as a ransom for many."*

It couldn't be said any clearer. Jesus came to serve and to give. It makes sense then that God desires the same for His disciples. After bringing us into His family through faith in His Son, the Lord sets His sights on building into us the same quality that made Jesus distinct from all the people of His day - a giving, servant-heart.

There is nothing more refreshing than a serving heart and a giving spirit. But it is as rare as diamonds too. Such a heart-attitude is the exception rather than the rule in our society and sadly, even in the church. Our selfish old nature continues to rare it's ugly head and demand attention. I am encouraged to know that even the first disciples; even those who sat at Jesus' feet; even those who walked, talked and lived with the greatest servant of all; even they struggled with this.

Let me give you one example. On this occasion our Lord's popularity was on the rise, the knowledge of His Kingdom was spreading and the disciples began to be anxious about being recognised as members of His chosen band. What makes this account a little more interesting is the presence of the mother of two disciples. She is the wife of Zebedee – the Galilean fisherman and the mother of James and John.

> **Matthew 20:20-24** *"Then the mother of Zebedee's sons came to Jesus with her sons and, kneeling down, asked a favour of him. "What is it you want?" he asked. She said, "Grant that one of these two sons of mine may sit at your right and the other at your left in your kingdom."*
>
> *"You don't know what you are asking," Jesus said to them. "Can you drink the cup I am going to drink?"*
>
> *"We can," they answered. Jesus said to them, "You will indeed drink from my cup, but to sit at my right or left is not for me to grant. These places belong to those for whom they have been prepared by my Father." When the ten heard about this, they were indignant with the two brothers."*

Now don't be too tough on this dear Jewish mum. She's very proud of her sons and she had obviously thought about that request for some time.

Her motive was probably pure and her idea was in proper perspective. She didn't ask that her sons occupy the centre throne - of course not - that belonged to Jesus. But like any good mother who watches out for the breaks in life that could lead to a nice promotion, she pushes her James and John forward as candidates for thrones 2 and 3. She wanted to enhance their image. She wanted people to think highly of her boys who had left their jobs and entered this up-and-coming ministry. They were among the first twelve and that needed recognition.

As can be seen from verse 24, the other ten were tarred with the same brush. They became indignant. Why? Because there was no way they were going to give up those top spots without a fight. They were ticked off that James and John might get the glory they wanted. Sound familiar?

With biting conviction Jesus answers the mother in verse 22 when He said: *"You do not know what you are asking."* That must have stunned her. She really thought she did. She used all of the world's ideas about authority and status to ask this question. But she was to discover that this movement was not of this world.

Jesus pulls His disciples aside and spells out the sharp contrast between His philosophy and the world system in which they lived.

> **Matthew 20:25-28** *Jesus called them together and said, "You know that the rulers of the Gentiles lord it over them, and their high officials exercise authority over them. Not so with you. Instead, whoever wants to become great among you must be your servant, and whoever wants to be first must be your slave - just as the Son of Man did not come to be served, but to serve, and to give his life as a ransom for many."*

In the secular world there are distinct levels of authority. Today in government we have the Prime Minister and His cabinet and a large body of personally selected men and women who have privileges that the common citizen does not enjoy.

In the military there are officers and enlisted men and women and ranks within each category. In sport there are coaches and players. In the business world there are corporation heads and lines of authority between managers and personnel, foremen and labourers.

The person in the labour force is expected to show up on time, punch a clock, work hard and not take advantage of his or her employer. There is a name for those who choose to not follow those clear directions - unemployed! Why? Because the boss is in charge and that's the way it works.

But Jesus says to His disciples and to us: *"not so among you."* What isn't so? Simply this: in God's family there is one great body of people standing on level ground before the cross of Christ and they all have the same title: *servant.* In fact, if there is any hierarchy in the kingdom of God; if there is any status or importance or greatness in the kingdom of God; it comes through being the best servant. Jesus said if we want to be great in God's kingdom we become the servant of all.

These seem to be forgotten words in our society and even in many churches today. With our smooth Pastors and high-powered executives and superstar up-front performers, unfortunately the servant mentality is not that common. We tend to get so caught up in the success and numbers game, we lose sight of our primary calling as followers of the Servant King. The celebrity syndrome, so dominant in our western Christian culture, doesn't even resemble the attitude and message of Jesus.

Colossians 1:15-18 *"The Son is the image of the invisible God, the firstborn over all creation. For in him all things were created: things in heaven and on earth, visible and invisible, whether thrones or powers or rulers or authorities; all things have been created through him and for him. He is before all things, and in him all things hold together. And he is the head of the body, the church; he is the beginning and the firstborn from among the dead, so that in everything he might have the supremacy."*

In the body of Christ there is only one Head - Jesus Christ. No other human being dare take that position. The rest of us are all servants. Yes, we have leadership roles and there is God-given authority attached to many of those roles, but the people holding those positions are still servants in the first instance. We are all called to be servants first - those other roles, functions and gifts must all be exercised in the context of serving - or they are not consistent with the clear revelation of what it is to be a disciple of Jesus.

This is so hard to do when we live in a world dominated by three words: I - ME - MINE. Those words stand out in bold print. They dominate our speech and our attitudes and are part of the very fabric of our culture. A series of television adds a few years ago bombarded us with the statement that the most important person in the world is you. That sums up the self-absorbed focus of our society. It's everyone for themselves. The prevailing attitude is, *'look after No. 1 - because nobody else will.'*

There is no doubt about it, this unhealthy focus on self is so engrained in our culture that it has also permeated church life, and we need to face it head on. If we are to pursue the road of discipleship; if we are to truly follow Jesus and walk in His steps; then we must face this servant test every day.

Philippians 2:3-4 *"Do nothing out of selfish ambition or vain conceit. Rather, in humility value others above yourselves, not looking to your own interests but each of you to the interests of the others."*

What a different story we get from the world. Look at the sporting world where billions of dollars are poured into one goal: proving our superiority over others. Apart from all the social and health benefits of sport, which are very positive, at the very heart of the world of competitive sport there is selfishness, pride and arrogance which all feed our ego and hinder our ability to live as servants. I am sure there are some humble champions, but they are somewhat rare.

I know that sport is a sacred cow in this nation and I know my comments may not rest with some sports fans. But I challenge you to build a theology of competitive sport out of the New Testament. Many have tried and failed. Paul uses some sporting analogies a couple of times to make a point, and people try to use that to justify competitive sport.

I've been down this road before. I wrote a small book decades ago entitled: *Living as a Christian in a Competitive World.* It was not a best seller! Many who read it - didn't like it at all because it challenged sacred cows like sport and education methods and business practices that millions of Christians are involved in. It was very threatening, but I believe my challenge came from the New Testament. We can ignore it and say it's too hard, or we can seriously ask the question: how can I be a servant of all in everything I do.

The business world in no better. Everywhere you look it's dog-eat-dog and fierce competition. Some of that is healthy, as different people do the same thing in different ways, giving the consumers a choice. If the market is big enough for several players, then let them have a go.

But a lot of it is very unhealthy. When companies have the primary goal of dominating the market, pushing all other competitors out of the industry, they are always winning at someone else's expense.

The education system has also suffered the same fate. The system of grading that has been in place over the last 100 years or so sets students against each other, competing for a mark on a piece of paper. The educators are quick to tell us how successful this method is in motivating students to do well. But they are not so quick to tell us at what cost.

When we have generations of people brainwashed into thinking that their worth is measured by their performance against a pre-determined academic standard and that they have to beat everyone else to get anywhere in life, what kind of society has that produced?   Look around and see!

How is it possible for Christians to be servants in such an environment? We run to the church for protection and find that the same selfishness dominates our life together as Christians.

We choose to worship in a church that meets our needs. If we like the worship, the Pastor and the teaching, then we stay. If any of that changes, and is not to our liking, then we withdraw; we judge; we complain and eventually we leave. Little thought is given to what we can *give* to that church body – we focus only on what we can *get.*

Our needs, our desires and our preferences too often inform all our decisions. In the very place we should expect to find this servant attitude (the church), we find that selfishness and pride are also present and now the difference between us and those outside the church is barely noticeable.

Jesus said: *"If you want to be great in God's kingdom - you must be the servant of all."* That word 'all' means everyone around you. I don't really need to give you examples in your family, your church, your workplace or in your neighbourhood.

Every single day we are confronted with the same choice: to serve ourselves and our needs and desires or serve others. It's when we make the wrong choice in this servant test that things start to fall apart in all our relationships. Think how harmonious your workplace would be if everyone had as their primary goal, serving the needs of others. What a great place to work!

Most marriage problems arise because one or both partners start to assert their needs and don't serve the needs of their spouse. If we entered marriage with only one goal: to serve the other person totally and completely forever, then our marriages would be fail-safe. If both partners have a servant-heart, they will be satisfied, fulfilled and have a solid marriage.

The tricky thing is that when one partner starts to lose that servant-heart, the other one feels justified in letting go their commitment to serve too. That's not how it supposed to be at all. We make a commitment to serve our partner's needs above our own no matter what the circumstances. That can be really tough at times, but if the marriage is to survive the ups and downs of life, that attitude must remain.

Think of how great the church would be if everyone came to give to each other and not take from each other. Think of how many people would want to be Pastors and leaders of a group of people like that. It would be like heaven on earth. If everyone - including the leaders - had as their primary goal and motivation – serving the needs of others - what a place it would be!

Well, I think you already know that the New Testament says that's what every church fellowship should look like - gatherings of people with servant-hearts who build one another up, encourage one another, serve one another and love one another. That is the New Testament model of the church and if we are serious about travelling the road of a true disciple; if we are serious about digesting the meat of the kingdom of God, then dealing with this important issue of servanthood must be high on our priority list.

Perhaps it is time we took a long hard look at our servant-hearts this coming week as we allow the Spirit of God to show us those areas where we can serve others' needs above our own - in our marriage, our family, our workplace, our neighbourhood and especially our church family.

Songwriter Graham Kendrick said it best: *"So let us learn how to serve, each other's needs to prefer, for it is Christ we're serving."* We will only learn how to serve as we let go of our own needs and desires and let God meet those directly or through others; ask for His empowering presence; ask for the grace to serve others.

We cannot do this in our own strength. Only by grace can we stand and only by grace can we serve.

6. THE SERVANT TEST (2)

As we continue our study in discipleship, I want to pick up where I left off in chapter 6. As we've been discovering in this book, there are many tests we must face on this discipleship road. Some of them confront us every day and we have choices as to how we respond to those tests. With many of them, we need to face them head on in the strength and courage of the Lord and pass them if we are to journey on any further and digest any of the real 'meat' of the kingdom of God. We've looked at the submission test, the obedience test and we've started looking at the servant test. I want to say some more about that test now because I believe it is one that that lies at the very core our Christian faith and practice and one that we face every day in every area of our lives.

We have been reminded that Jesus Himself is the ultimate example of a servant. As Paul tells us in Philippians 2, Jesus made a choice to be a servant. He chose to set aside His divinity, His status, His glory and His exalted position at the right hand of the Father and made a deliberate choice to step out of eternity and into time when He became one of us in order to serve us.

Many years before that, Isaiah prophesied this event and said that He would be a lowly, humble, suffering servant, not an exalted king on his throne in a castle surrounded by an army of thousands, but a lowly servant, walking the dusty streets of the Middle East, always putting the needs of others above His own.

Towards the end of His time among us, Jesus took a hand basin and towel and washed his followers' feet. When He did that, He made a very powerful statement about who He was and who we are to be if we want to follow Him.

The Son of Man did not come to be served but to serve and give His life as a ransom for many. We were challenged in the last chapter to look at our own lives and identify those areas where we can serve others' needs above our own. I want us to examine this even further now as the Spirit reminds us again of our role as a servant.

Warren Wiersbe, one of the twentieth century's greatest preachers and teachers, had a definition of ministry which I believe is worth memorising:

Ministry takes place when Divine resources meet human needs through loving channels to the glory of God.

If you and I desire to be ministers of the gospel; if we desire to be obedient disciples of the Lord Jesus Christ, then we must first of all know and experience those divine resources personally. We must be connected to the power of the living God. Only then will we be able to see the human needs around us with understanding and compassion and be the loving channels God needs to meet those needs. And all of this is done for one reason - the glory of God. When God is glorified, His Spirit can work to bring Christ to those who need to know Him.

At the heart of the above definition is the understanding that ministry is for others. We are called as Christians to live for others. As I have already said, we all have the same role: servant. Ministry is not just another way of filling in our time or making a living if you are full time. It is a wonderful opportunity to make a life that is lived for others. It is an opportunity to live and minister and serve like the Lord Jesus; to see His life and character and mission develop and grow in us and affect all that we think, say and do.

When Jesus was here on earth, He met all kinds of human needs and He wasn't always thanked or appreciated. Some even turned against Him. We live in a world filled with people who have incredible needs of all kinds.

There are a number of ways we can relate to these needs. It's a choice that each of us faces every day as we observe those needs. We may choose to be blind to them as we live our own lives and serve our own interests. That is an option many of us choose. It goes directly against our calling as a disciple, but it's still an option we can choose. Again, the Lord Jesus leads the way here. Paul reminds us in Philippians 2 of the character of Jesus and the character we are called to exhibit when he wrote this:

> **Philippians 2:3-4** *"Do nothing out of selfish ambition or vain conceit. Rather, in humility value others above yourselves, not looking to your own interests but each of you to the interests of the others."*

We can be blind to those needs at times, but I doubt that we want to be like that. We may choose to take advantage of those needs for our own benefit. Yes, sadly, it is possible to be in ministry and use people to get what we want instead of helping people to get what they need.

The Pharisees were a prime example here. They used the people to build their own authority and importance. Jesus exposed this in Matthew 23.

If we are not careful, we can minister in such a way that we exploit the needs of others to get ourselves recognition, position, status or privileges. True servants will always help others whether they benefit from that serving or not. They are only concerned that people's needs are met and that God is glorified in the process.

Or we may know about the needs of others but choose to do nothing. That's exactly what the Priest and the Levite did when they saw the dying man on the road in the parable of the Good Samaritan. Both saw the needs of the man but chose to pass by on the other side. Granted, it is impossible as a servant of God for us to do something about every need we encounter. But that should never be used as an excuse to do nothing about any of them!

We all know that we should not turn a blind eye to the needs of others; nor should we exploit them; nor should we ignore them. The only way for a true servant to respond is to ask: *'Lord, what can I do to be a loving channel for this person so that they can connect with Your resources?'*

Let me put it in worldly terms: **we are not called to be manufacturers - we are called to be distributors.** God is the one with the products, it's God's love, God's grace, God's mercy, God's wisdom, God's strength, God's power, God's guidance and God's word. People desperately need all of them! We have nothing that will meet their needs. We can only act as distributors of what God has for them. We are called to be loving channels through which God can pour Himself into the lives of others.

That should take the heat off us a little. We don't have to *make* anything happen. We don't have to even have the answers to people's problems. We just need to be there for them, with open hearts, compassion and understanding – as we allow God to do the rest.

The people we are called to serve, have all kinds of needs: physical, emotional, relational, financial; but at the heart of it all, their greatest need is God. That doesn't mean that the Word of God or prayer will pay their bills or fill their stomachs directly.

We don't quote a Bible promise to a hungry person and send them on their way with an empty stomach. No, we must do what we can to meet those immediate human needs. But unless we also help people grow into a right relationship with God, whatever help we give will only be temporary; a band-aid measure; a stopgap; a quick fix until the next time they have a need and the cycle is repeated.

Perhaps that's one of the main differences between genuine Christian ministry and mere humanitarian benevolence, as helpful as it may be. Both can be done in love; both can put food on the table and shoes on the feet; but only true Christian ministry can put grace in the heart so that lives are transformed and people's deepest problems are solved.

The best way to truly serve someone is not to solve their problems for them, but to lead them to God's grace, His empowering presence in their lives, so they will be able to solve all their problems in His strength and His power – not their own, and not yours.

Somebody once said: *at the heart of every problem is the problem of the heart.* But this statement is only partly true because sometimes it's not what we have done, but what others have done to us. Children sometimes suffer for what their parents do.

The opposite can also be true. The company manager embezzles money and wrecks the business and dozens of innocent workers are out on the streets looking for work. They did nothing wrong. People may not cause their own problems, but they will most certainly make them worse if they relate to their problems the wrong way.

What life does to us depends on what life finds in us. That is where the grace of God comes in.

The church is the Body of Christ on earth. We are the day-to-day manifestation of Jesus Christ. We are the only Jesus many people are going to see and hear. So, we must project the real Jesus, the suffering servant of all, the one Who did not come to be served but to serve and give His life as a ransom for many. That is to be our attitude. Our hearts are to be giving, servant hearts - sacrifice and service, to the glory of God. Selfishness says: *what will I get?* Service says: *what I have I will give to you freely.* Human needs today are countless and indescribable and if you have a tender heart, almost unbearable. You and I can't do everything, but we can do something, and that something is the ministry that God has called us to fulfil.

I came across a new word in my reading this week. The word is *Erinaceous*. It is a zoological term which describes the Hedgehog family. I believe some people are erinaceous! They are like hedgehogs - the closer you get to them, the more you are wounded by their protective quills. You want to help them, but if you do, you are going to get hurt.

If the motivation for our serving is anything less that Christ's love rising up in our hearts, then our ministry will not really meet human needs long-term, and it most certainly won't glorify God. When Jesus saw the multitude in Matthew 9, He was moved with compassion for them. That's why Paul said in 2 Corinthians 5:14 that the love of Christ compels us - or constrains us.

When I use the term 'loving channels' I don't mean to imply that God's servants are passive conduits through whom God pours His blessings, come what may. God doesn't want to work *in spite of us* or *instead of us*, He wants to work *in us and through us*. Then, as He is working to share His divine resources, in partnership with us, to bless someone else, He blesses 'the channel' in the process.

If a worker doesn't get a blessing out of the work, something is radically wrong. Serving in the kingdom of God isn't punishment, it's nourishment. Jesus said: *"My food is to do the will of Him who sent me and to do His work."*

Serving in the Kingdom of God requires us to work with people and people not only *have* problems, they can often *be* the problems because of the way they deal with the issues they face. They can grow invisible protective quills to keep others at a distance and if you don't genuinely love these people in the Lord, you will never be able to help them.

Some people are blind to their own needs and constantly want to go on a detour from the real issue they are facing. Other people choose to ignore their needs completely and blame somebody else.

Then there are people who have learned to exploit their needs to get what they want from others. They can't afford to have their problems solved because their whole lifestyle is built on them! This third group is the hardest to help.

We must remember nevertheless that we are loving channels of the grace of God. As Bernard of Clairveaux once said: *'Justice seeks out the merits of the case, love only regards the need.'* We who are servants, don't deserve His grace any more than those we are serving. Who are we to limit God's grace and mercy just because we don't like how a person is responding?

We must always keep grace and truth in balance, however. There is never a situation when the truth of who God is and what He has called us to do and to be, can be overlooked in our service of others. Jesus loved people all the way to cross, but He also confronted error along the way. If grace and truth contradict one another, then something is amiss.

Now many of us confess that we are simply not capable of loving people the way Jesus does. We do our best to practice 1 Corinthians 13, but it doesn't always last. However, that is the manufacturer mentality once again. God does not ask us to work up this love in our own strength. He promises to pour His love into us when we need it. The love of God has been poured out in our hearts by the Holy Spirit who has been given to us (Romans 5:5).

The love that we need for ministry and to be a true disciple and servant of God, is not a natural ability. It is a supernatural gift only God can give.

When the people we serve irritate us or disappoint us or attack us, the first thing we usually do is pray for them and ask the Lord to change them. What we ought to do first is to pray for ourselves and ask God to increase His love in us – for that is what will ultimately change others.

Ephesians 4:32 exhorts us to be kind to one another (even if they are not kind to us), be tender-hearted (even if they hurt us), forgive one another even as God in Christ forgave us. The Holy Spirit can make us adequate for any ministry challenge He brings our way. If fact, I believe God allows some problem people to come into our lives so we will learn to depend more on His power than our own resources.

There is a truth about Christian service that many of us overlook, it is simply this: God is as concerned about the servant as He is the service. If God's sole agenda was to get the work done, He could just send His angels, they would do a far better job in much less time. But you see God not only wants to do something *through* us, He also wants to do something *in* us. That is why the hedgehogs show up in our lives. God uses them to encourage us to pray and to trust in Him and to depend on His Spirit for love and grace.

We will always have EGR people in our life *(Extra Grace Required)* and we know that this grace can only come from God. Difficult people and difficult circumstances can be used by the Spirit of God to help us grow and become more like Christ. Too often, however, when these difficulties come, our tendency is to pray for deliverance instead of growth, maturity and strength. We ask the Lord: *"How can I get out of this?"* instead of: *"What can I learn from this?"* When we do that, we miss the opportunities that God gives us to grow and mature.

I have learned the hardest possible way that when such circumstances or people come against me, I need to ask: *"Where are You in this Lord?"* Not, *"Are You in this?"* Because I know He is. I need to be strong enough to ask Him, *"What are You doing with this situation? What is it You are trying to say to me, in and through this expedience?"* I used to pray: *"Lord, get me out of here fast!"* I now try to pray: *"Lord use me in this situation to do Your will and allow me to grow and mature in the process."*

Often you will feel like quitting and running away, but that's the worst thing you can do. Running away will never solve your problems or meet the true needs. You will just meet the same situation and the same people, with different names in the next chapter of your journey, because God won't let His servants run away. He is determined that His children are conformed to the image of His Son, and so He will keep working on us until He accomplishes His goal.

It's only human to want to run away from a tough situation. But brothers and sisters, it is always too soon to quit. You will meet problem people and problem situations wherever you go, so make up your mind now to expect them, accept them and let God use them in your life as you continue to be His servant and theirs.

The devil wants to use those 'porcupines' and 'EGRS' as weapons to tear you down, but the Spirit can use them as tools to build you up. It's your choice which will happen. If you persevere and endure and trust God to work, you'll experience His grace in a wonderful way and you'll be a better servant.

In Christian ministry, problems with people are among the most difficult to bear, and the people who have and who cause the greatest problems are those who need us the most. That's why we need to be channels of God's love and grace - no matter how people may respond to our ministry. It may take years before they allow the Lord to change them and you may not even be around when it happens. That doesn't matter, because the Lord is on the job, and He will finish what He has begun and He will receive the glory.

The same Jesus Who said, *"Follow me,"* also said, *"If you want to be great in the kingdom of God, you must be the servant of all."* But as I wrap up this chapter, let me stress again, if it's not a joy for you to serve, then something is wrong. If it's not a blessing, something is wrong. If your service, as hard and painful as it may be at times, is not fulfilling, rewarding and satisfying then something is wrong in your heart.

Service is tough. Ask Jesus how tough it can be, and He will stretch out His hands on the cross and say, *"This tough!"* But it will also be a blessing and a joy. Which is why it says in Hebrews that *it was for the joy set before Him, that Jesus endured the cross.* He can, and He will give us that same servant heart and that same joy.

7. THE GIVING TEST

As we have journeyed down the discipleship road in this study we have encountered various tests. The submission test, the obedience test, and over the last two chapters we have been looking at the servant test.

Now I want to look at another test which we face every day and which also lies at the heart of the New Testament concept of the Christian life. It is also one of the hardest tests to face in our self-centred 'looking-after-No.1' society. I refer to the giving test.

Of course, the moment I mention the word *giving*, the vast majority of people immediately think of money, and yet I am sure you know by now that giving involves far more than just money. But whenever that word is mentioned from a pulpit, we nearly always think of money.

Well, I am not going to specifically talk about money at all in this chapter. I want us to look at giving in a far broader and deeper context. Giving lies at the heart of our Christian experience and it can unlock so many doors in the kingdom of God.

When I talk about giving, I am not talking about the outward action which can be carried out with little or no feeling. I am talking about the heart attitude that gives the right thing at the right time in the right way and for the right reasons. Our giving can take many different forms.

There are times to *give up* - not in resignation, abandonment or despair, but in surrender. Not a day goes by when we are not called in some way to give up our sense of importance and position for the sake of others and the kingdom.

Then there are times to *forgive* - to release what would be retained as a grudge or anger or as pain or as resentment or as internalised stress as a result of a perceived or a real injustice. We may not see forgiveness as part of the giving test, but it lies at the heart of this test. One of the hardest things we are called upon to give is the grace of forgiveness, particularly when we have been genuinely wronged.

I remember my wife attended a Jim Glennon seminar many years ago and she came home with a statement that we have both referred to many times over the years. Jim said: *"The devil of resentment is that it's justified."* There are so many situations which we will face on this discipleship road where we are justifiably hurt or angry because of what has been done to us. Our need to give at a point like that is so essential – we must give up all resentment.

Then there are times to *give over* - to place into the hands of the Creator-judge of the universe, matters that only His might and His justice can sufficiently handle. How tightly do you clutch onto some issues and problems in your life? What burdens are you carrying around right now, trying to ease through your own effort? Why not just give them over to the Lord?

There are also times to *give to.* This is when you take from your abundance and give to someone with a greater need. The Bible makes it very clear that if we see a brother or sister in need and choose to do nothing about that need, then there is no love in us.

Opportunities to give to others surround us every day. We are called to give out of our abundance. We are so blessed in this nation. I know many of us have financial struggles at times, but compared to millions of others who share this planet with us, we have an abundance of everything.

There are also times to *give in* through simple obedience. Our wise God has shown us principles and patterns of giving as a discipline, intending to release us from a self-centred survival mindset or from our all-too-human self-protecting fear of want or poverty.

There are also times to *give wisely* because we understand the reciprocal laws of the kingdom of God which promise a bountiful return as we give. That's God's encouragement for us to learn to give over and over and over again with increasing resources and joyfulness. We don't give in order to get something back, but the fact remains that in the God's kingdom, giving is reciprocated by God in abundance.

In short, giving involves everything, but never the way we most fear. Fear has taught us that to give something means we are left with less, and therefore, to give everything is to be left with nothing. This self-centred protection mindset is a sickness directly related to our fallen, sinful nature and when we are born again in our spirits to God, we should let go of this insatiable desire to *keep* as we let an even stronger desire to *give* replace it.

Of course, all this takes time. We don't lose our ego-centric selfishness overnight. Our new life in the kingdom will take time to grow. Biologically, nine months in the womb and a dozen or so years following birth are just the beginning of the growth of a human being who can think about or care for anyone other than themselves. Similarly, our spiritual new birth in Christ is only a starting place for growth in a lifetime of learning to live in the spirit of God's grace.

God's releasing grace is that grace in life that compels us to give as we have received, forgive as we have been forgiven and care for and serve others as God cares for and serves us in His Son Jesus.

Those words: *the spirit of God's releasing grace,* create the foundation of all giving. They draw their truth from the highest principle of all, and that is: *love gives.* They are rooted in God's love which is the foremost of all God's attributes. It is God's love that mandates His giving and forgiving, because His nature can do nothing else. It is also His love that mandates that those who are born into His family learn to do the same.

This principle lies at the very heart of one of Jesus' most revealing parables. Jesus presents it as a kingdom parable by saying that the kingdom of God is like this.

> **Matthew 18:23-35** *"Therefore, the kingdom of heaven is like a king who wanted to settle accounts with his servants. As he began the settlement, a man who owed him ten thousand bags of gold was brought to him. Since he was not able to pay, the master ordered that he and his wife and his children and all that he had be sold to repay the debt.*
>
> *"At this the servant fell on his knees before him. 'Be patient with me,' he begged, 'and I will pay back everything.' The servant's master took pity on him, cancelled the debt and let him go.*
>
> *"But when that servant went out, he found one of his fellow servants who owed him a hundred silver coins. He grabbed him by the throat and began to choke him. 'Pay back what you owe me!' he demanded. His fellow servant fell to his knees and begged him, 'Be patient with me, and I will pay it back.'*
>
> *"But he refused. Instead, he went off and had the man thrown into prison until he could pay the debt. When the other servants saw what had happened, they were outraged and went and told their master everything that had happened.*

"Then the master called the servant in. 'You wicked servant,' he said, 'I cancelled all that debt of yours because you begged me to. Shouldn't you have had mercy on your fellow servant just as I had on you?' In anger his master handed him over to the jailers to be tortured, until he should pay back all he owed.

"This is how my heavenly Father will treat each of you unless you forgive your brother or sister from your heart."

I said earlier on that our challenge as disciples is to learn to give the right things in the right way at the right time for the right reasons. Jesus' teaching in this vivid story deals with all those "right" things. He gives us a vital lesson in forgiveness which reveals the need for forgiving others, for giving up selfish interest and giving into God's greater wisdom.

At the very heart of this story lies the reason for such a mandate for forgiveness. We need to understand the right reason for giving. This is crucial, because giving is not a wand we wave in some magical way. It is an attitude worked into the human heart through understanding God's heart and purposes. The pivotal point in Jesus' whole teaching here is at the central moment in the confrontation between the forgiving master and the unforgiving servant.

Jesus' message is clear and pointed: **forgotten grace breeds unforgiving living.** His analogy is so clear. The picture of God's greatness and grace in forgiving each of us our sins through the cross of Jesus is clearly in view in the master's release of his debt-ridden servant. This is the reason, the pivot point, the powerbase from which our giving springs. Jesus makes the gift of God's love and salvation a starting point for all our learning about giving.

Whether mercy or money, forgiveness or resources, we must first of all receive and understand His grace as the fountainhead of our lives if we are to grow at all in our ability to give. The foundational elements of that growth are in the parable you have just read.

The context of Jesus telling this story is significant. Peter had just expressed what to him seemed to be a gracious offer. *"Lord, should I forgive people seven times?"* Peter was stretching way past the common expectation in his day for forgiveness. The school of thought present in religion at that time proposed that even God didn't forgive people more than three times. This had been deduced from the writings of the Prophet Amos. Some Rabbis had concluded that God forgave a transgression three times but when a fourth violation occurred, judgement would strike. So, when Peter suggested that he should forgive seven times, it ought to be noted that he would have considered this to be very generous. The response Jesus gave would have therefore stunned Peter and all those with him. Jesus said: *"Not seven, but seventy times seven!"*

Now Jesus was not addressing fools here. They recognised immediately what He meant. He didn't expect them to keep tabs on forgiveness for each person and when you get to 490 times, then you can let them have it. No, the figure He gave was meant to be so outrageously high that people realised what He was really saying and that is that our forgiveness should be unrelenting. *"Never stop forgiving,"* is what He was saying. Jesus was describing what true love does. As we see in 1 Corinthians 13, love does not keep any record of wrongs - it *always* forgives. Then to drive the point home even further Jesus told a profoundly simple story, yet gave us a marvellously complete picture of the salvation God offers each one of us in Christ. It clearly illustrates seven important truths.

1. We are all God's created, accountable servants.
2. Our debt is our sin which are greater than we can repay.
3. Our destiny is doomed because of our debt.
4. Our cry for God's mercy when uttered will always find a compassionate response.
5. His forgiveness is total and unconditional.
6. Our debt is cancelled through Christ's life, death and resurrection.
7. Having been forgiven completely, we are expected to live in the same way towards others.

Therefore, central to Jesus' call to live a life of giving and forgiving is the truth that our debt before God has been paid freely by Him and Him alone. He has done all of this notwithstanding our responsibility for our sins and our inability to pay for them.

In this lesson Jesus shows us the majesty and totality of God's forgiveness. It is the substance which forms the very foundation of all of life; life now; life eternal; and life to be lived in and through God's amazing grace.

In order to establish this foundation for our lives it is crucial that we sense the need of the servant in Jesus' parable. His problem was his debt, which is an analogy for our sinful human condition. He was helpless and hopeless. He had no point of appeal to excuse himself from his debt. It was real and it was unpayable.

His words, *"Give me time"* only point to the incredible way our flesh will plead for its own potential power to answer our problems. In today's currency this debt would be in the vicinity of 100 million dollars and the man is just a common wage earner on the equivalent of a labourer's salary. This debt was completely beyond his means. That's the whole point of the story!

If we are to gain a hold in this ministry and lifestyle of giving and forgiving, we must never, ever forget our true condition outside Christ. Forgetfulness feeds our inability to see ourselves in the need or failing of other people. The servant's actions to the one who owes him money seem unimaginable until we observe our own unforgiveness. Look at these words and watch the actions of this 'just-having-been-forgiven-a-fortune' servant.

> **Matthew 18:28** *"But when that servant went out, he found one of his fellow servants who owed him a hundred silver coins. He grabbed him by the throat and began to choke him. 'Pay back what you owe me!' he demanded.*

The picture couldn't be more graphic. Some translations say, *"By the throat."* Something about this man's violence shakes our sensitivities as we look at the absolute insanity of the horrible forgetfulness that manifests. The inability of the forgiven servant to translate his blessing into similar grace for another, causes us to rise up in indignant defence. Everything in us screams out against this brutal man.

But the purpose of this confronting text isn't to incite our anger for anyone other than ourselves. However guiltless we may plead to be, we have all been guilty of this same forgetfulness. Because we probably didn't grab someone by the throat and demand money, we may not immediately see ourselves in this story. But the same spirit of unforgiveness is present:

… when we criticise a brother or sister.
… when we judgementally condemn a gross sinner.
… when we feel vindictive against an enemy.
… when we speak unkindly to a relative.
… when we reject someone who does not fit our social taste or preconditions.

…   when we tolerate condescending attitudes towards people of different ethnic backgrounds.

…   when we attack fellow Christians for practices or positions that are different from ours.

…   when we mock any human being or carry hatred or anger towards another person.

The list goes on. In short, virtually every clash in our human relationships is due to some expression of an unwillingness to give, to forgive or to give understanding concerning our differences.

The relatively small debt of the second servant is another key part of Jesus message. In contrast to the unpayable millions constituting the first servant's debt, 100 denarii would equate to about $40.00 - an amount that could have been paid back over a relatively short time.

> **Matthew 18:29** *His fellow servant fell to his knees and begged him, 'Be patient with me, and I will pay it back.'*

You would think that the first servant would have been shaken awake by those words. They were a precise echo of the request he had made to his master. But he had been asking for time to pay millions - not just $40.00. Now, when he receives a reasonable request from someone for extra time to pay back an infinitely smaller debt, he's totally oblivious to his fellow-servant's plea for patience.

There are drastic differences in the way the two appeals were handled. In the first instance the master had great compassion and forgave him the debt and let him go. This was done in the face of an impossible amount and yet the requirement of payment was totally removed. In the second instance the forgiven servant cast his fellow-servant into the debtor's prison, disallowing the opportunity of repayment.

The human parallels are again obvious. How soon we all forget the greatness of God's grace which looked beyond our faults and seeing our needs - totally forgave us. How easily we fall prey to hasty judgement. How slow we are to measure the relative failure of those who may violate us against the backdrop of our own violations against God. Our sin seems too small in comparison.

Yet in the midst of all of this, Jesus calls us to accountability as He reminds us to never forget the dimensions of our deliverance and God's forgiveness. Jesus says this is how it is in the kingdom of God, and if we desire to live as the kingdom people we claim to be; if we want to truly follow Jesus; then we will face this giving test every day in so many ways, because this is the reality of God's kingdom.

Jesus has come to bring heaven's rule and reign into our hearts right now. The forgiven are called to forgive. Those to whom so much has been given are called to give out their abundance. To the same degree that we have been entirely, unconditionally and graciously forgiven - we are to forgive others. To the same degree that we have been blessed abundantly and share in the riches of heaven - we are to bless others and allow them to share all that we have.

We need to understand however that none of us are going to even come close to passing this giving test if we are not connected with the giving grace of God. Clearly, this is not something that we can do in the flesh. We don't just make a resolution to be giving people. Until the spirit of God's releasing grace connects with and saturates our spirit; until we embrace the reality, the magnitude and the power of the grace, love and forgiveness of God; we will not have the spiritual resources to give or forgive in any way at all. Each of us needs to get on our knees before God and ask for a fresh revelation of His grace, mercy, love and forgiveness.

If we don't remain in daily contact with the power of His grace and the magnitude of what He has given us, we will not be able to live a life of giving.

The only reason that we have such a death grip on our money, time and abundant resources, is because we don't fully appreciate the truth that everything we are, everything we have and everything we ever hope to be has come through the grace of God; we don't accept that outside of Jesus Christ, in Whose righteousness we stand, we have and we are absolutely nothing!

When the reality of that truth births afresh in our spirit, we will find it very hard *not* to give. For when the giving love and grace of God saturates our being, it will automatically overflow into the lives of all those who encounter us.

8. THE TRUST TEST

I want to begin this chapter by reminding you of a very well-known passage from Proverbs and one that contains a vitally important truth for all disciples of the Lord. We are given the promise that the Lord will direct our paths if we trust in Him.

> **Proverbs 3:5-6** *"Trust in the Lord with all your heart and lean not on your own understanding; in all your ways submit to him, and he will make your paths straight."*

Jeremiah 17:7 says that the one who trusts in the Lord and places their confidence in Him, will be blessed. Then in 1 Chronicles 5:20 we are told that God answers the prayers of those who trust in Him. In Romans 15:13 Paul implies that God will fill us with joy and peace and that we will overflow with hope by the power of the Holy Spirit if we trust in Him. In fact, if you do a word study on *trust* in the Bible you will find hundreds of references from Genesis to Revelation. The issue of trust lies at the heart of our relationship with God.

In our journey down the discipleship road in this series, I believe the trust test is one of the most crucial and, like many of the tests we face, it is a daily challenge. Without question, we are called upon every single day to trust God in some way. In whom or in what do we place our trust each and every day as decisions are made; as issues are faced; as circumstances, good and bad, come our way? If we are honest and brave enough to evaluate where our trust lies, we may be found wanting some days. I believe at the heart of many challenges that face us as disciples of the Lord Jesus Christ, is this issue of trust.

The writer of Proverbs says we are to trust in the Lord *with all our heart,* which simply means with our whole being we are to trust Him and never should we lean on our own human understanding. But how many times each day do we face issues, people and circumstances and apply our own understanding and wisdom? How often do we turn to God first; and how many times is He pushed aside, only to be called upon when we can't work it out ourselves?

The Bible is full of warnings against trusting in anything but the Lord. In our affluent society, one of the things we can place our trust in without even knowing it, is our riches and wealth and our material possessions. If our trust in those things comes above our trust in the Lord - we are in trouble. You will recall the famous words in Psalm 20:7 which have been put to song more than once: *"Some trust in chariots, some in horses, but we will trust in the name of the Lord our God."*

Psalm 49:6 speaks against those who trust in their wealth and boast in their riches. Psalm 52:7 talks of the sad plight of the man who did not trust in God but rather in his wealth.

There is a strong warning in Psalm 62:10 where it says that even though our riches may increase, we are not to trust in them. Proverbs 11:28 is even more direct when it says whoever trusts in his riches will fall, but the righteous will thrive like a green leaf.

Now I am sure that we all know we are not to place our trust in riches, wealth or material possessions or those things made by the hand of man. We know it in theory, but what happens when those things disappear? It's easy to say we don't trust in wealth if we are wealthy. It's easy to say that we don't trust in material possessions we are blessed with so many. How do we stack up when they are gone?

The Bible also warns us against trusting in man. At times this becomes even harder because we have a great deal of respect for those around us and those in authority and even those we love and who are close to us. But we are warned that our ultimate trust must still be in the Lord. He is the only One we can be sure of in the final analysis. He is the only One Who cannot fail us and will never leave us. Only His love is unconditional and unfailing.

Psalm 9:10 says, *"Those who know Your name will trust in You for You O Lord have never forsaken those who seek You."* Psalm 13:5, *"I trust in your unfailing love and I rejoice in your salvation."* Psalm 40:4 says, *"Blessed is the man who makes the Lord his trust, who does not look to the proud or to those who turn aside to false gods."*

There are so many Bible references which compare man to God. Some of them are hard to swallow because we find it easier to trust someone with skin on; someone who is there in front of us each day. It takes faith and trust and courage to trust in an unseen God. But God is the only One Who has power over every single person, every problem and every circumstance. How often have we placed our trust in human beings only to discover they are powerless to help?

Psalm 118:8 is crystal clear when it says it is better to take refuge in the Lord than to trust in man. Proverbs 29:25 tells us that the trust of man will prove to be a snare, but whoever trusts in the Lord will be kept safe. Isaiah 2:22 says we should stop trusting in man who has but a breath in his nostrils, of what account is he?

Put your trust in the Lord. Jeremiah 17:5 is even more pointed when it says: *"Cursed is the one who trusts in man and who depends on flesh for his strength and whose heart turns away from the Lord."*

The strong inference here is that we have a choice between trusting man and trusting God. Now this doesn't mean for one moment that we immediately become suspicious of the people around us. Trust in the kingdom of God is essential. We must continue to give our trust to those around us - even when they betray it. That is the way of the kingdom. What I am talking about here is the underlying and undergirding trust that we must have in God alone, above and beyond any trust we have in human beings. In other words, our trust in another person must never come above our trust in God. Where does our highest allegiance lie? Is God the One to Whom we ultimately turn?

A good example of this is found in Acts 14:23 where Paul and Barnabas appointed elders in each Church. It says they appointed these men with prayer and fasting, committing them to the Lord in Whom they had put their trust. There is no doubt that these new elders had the trust of Paul and Barnabas or they would not have been appointed.

However, underlying that trust was Paul and Barnabas' trust in God. Regardless of the qualities and integrity of these men, they were still sinful, fallible humans who had the ability to fail and disobey and even turn on those who appointed them. Paul and Barnabas had to trust God more than they trusted these men. Only then could they make this appointment with peace in their heart knowing that God had it all in hand.

Behind our trust in any human relationship must still be our trust in the Lord. This applies to the appointment of Church leaders, the selection of our friends and even our marriage partners. In those decisions we make regarding who will lead us or who we will be friends with or who we will marry, if we don't trust God more than we trust those people or even ourselves, then we are in trouble.

Even more pointed than trusting in man generally, we are warned in Psalm 49:13 against trusting in ourselves and that includes trusting in our abilities and gifts and talents and the work that we do for God.

Speaking of Abraham and his faith, in Romans 4:4,5, Paul says: *"When a man works, his wages are not credited to him as a gift but as an obligation. However, to the man who does not work (in the power of the flesh) but trusts God who justifies even the wicked . . his faith is credited to him as righteousness."*

How often do you and I race off ahead of God without prayer; in our own strength; with own abilities; without His wisdom or guidance; only to find ourselves on the wrong path? It is true that God has blessed us with abilities, gifts, talents and experience, and we are to use those for His glory. However, we need to make sure that those things are used in a prayerful, careful, Spirit-directed manner.

If we stop trusting the giver of the gifts and start to trust the gifts themselves, we are in trouble. If we stop trusting the One Who gave us wisdom and all of our abilities and start trusting in those abilities and our wisdom alone, we are in trouble. We must trust in God and in God alone.

Our trust should never be in God's creation, including ourselves, including our own wisdom and knowledge and experience and gifts; our trust should always be in the One Who created all and sustains all by the power of His Word.

So, allow me to now put some meat on these bones and ask some pointed questions about trust.

In whom do you place your trust when circumstances change and your wealth or riches or possessions are taken away or lost?

In whom do you place your trust when you find yourself in a marriage that is less than perfect?

In whom do you place your trust when people oppose you or come against you?

In whom do you place your trust when the people who oppose you or come against you are friends or family?

In whom do you place your trust when you find yourself in disagreement with the boss at work, the lecturer at college, the teacher at school or even your own parents or adult children?

In whom do you place your trust when you find yourself in disagreement with your Pastor or Church leaders?

I could go on for a long time with examples. Our lives are full of them. The bottom-line question is this: *how big is the God you trust?*

Is He bigger than the tragedies of life that strike you? Ask Job.

Is He bigger than those who oppose you and attack you? Ask Stephen before he was stoned to death.

Is He bigger than your wealth and your possessions and those things this world offers you? Ask Job again.

Is He bigger than the pain of betrayal? Ask Jesus.

Is He bigger than the most oppressive leader? Ask David.

How big is your God? How powerful is your God? How much do you really trust Him in every area of your life? I know we are all fail in this area and I believe that we need to face the fact that what lies at the very heart of our lack of trust in God is the sin of unbelief – which really is the mother and father of all sins.

We don't trust God because we really don't believe He is who He says He is and that He can do what He says He can do. If we really believed that - we would find it easy to trust Him every day.

Hebrews 3:12-19 *"See to it, brothers and sisters, that none of you has a sinful, unbelieving heart that turns away from the living God. But encourage one another daily, as long as it is called "Today," so that none of you may be hardened by sin's deceitfulness. We have come to share in Christ, if indeed we hold our original conviction firmly to the very end. As has just been said:*

"Today, if you hear his voice, do not harden your hearts as you did in the rebellion."

Who were they who heard and rebelled? Were they not all those Moses led out of Egypt? And with whom was he angry for forty years? Was it not with those who sinned, whose bodies perished in the wilderness? And to whom did God swear that they would never enter his rest if not to those who disobeyed? So we see that they were not able to enter, because of their unbelief."

Romans 4:18-22 *Against all hope, Abraham in hope believed and so became the father of many nations, just as it had been said to him, "So shall your offspring be." Without weakening in his faith, he faced the fact that his body was as good as dead - since he was about a hundred years old - and that Sarah's womb was also dead.*

Yet he did not waver through unbelief regarding the promise of God, but was strengthened in his faith and gave glory to God, being fully persuaded that God had power to do what he had promised. This is why "it was credited to him as righteousness."

Belief lies at the heart of our faith. The world says, *"Show me the evidence and I will believe."* Faith says, *"I will choose to believe and then I will see the evidence."*

On this discipleship road, we must learn to trust God more than we trust ourselves, our friends, our experience, our money. Everything else must fall in behind our trust in God. That kind of trust is only possible when we believe that God is able to do all that He said He would do.

- *He will keep us safe.*
- *He will provide for our every need.*
- *He will vindicate us against our enemies in His way*
- *He will fulfil His plan and purpose through us*
- *He will build the Church that He promised to build.*

God will fulfil every last promise He has made to us, we just need to trust Him and not let any circumstance or any person get in the way of that total trust and confidence in Him. He knows how hard it is some days. Jesus has been there. Alone, cold, battered and friendless, Jesus climbed Calvary's hill and was tortured to death.

Jesus had to trust the Father to raise Him from the dead. The resurrection was essential if God's plan of salvation was to be fulfilled for us. Jesus died, trusting the Father to raise Him in three days. He had no guarantee – other than His trust in the Father.

Jesus knows how hard it is to trust God when everything around you tells you not to. He can identify with us at every point in this journey, and He will empower us to trust the Father like He did. His spirit will give us that ability, each and every day.

Many years ago now, a famous tightrope walker set up a cable across Niagara Falls and amazed crowds as he walked back and forth across the roaring waters below. The people cheered as he performed so many daring tricks - walking blindfolded, carrying a sack of potatoes, and even pushing a wheelbarrow across!

Then, he turned to the large crowd and asked, *"Do you believe I can push a person across in this wheelbarrow?"*

The people all enthusiastically shouted back to him, *"Yes! We believe!"*

Then he pointed to one man in the front and said to him, *"Great! Hop in."*

The man froze. He had believed the tightrope walker's words, but when it came to actually trusting him to do what he promised to do, fear held him back.

This is often how we are with God. We say we trust Him; we sing songs about faith; but when He asks us to fully surrender - whether it's with our future, our finances, or our fears - we hesitate. Genuine trust isn't just believing that God can take care of us; trust isn't just believing His Word, genuine trust is being willing to climb into the wheelbarrow and let Him do what He does!

> **Isaiah 26:3-4** *"You will keep in perfect peace those whose minds are steadfast, because they trust in you. Trust in the Lord forever, for the Lord, the Lord himself, is the Rock eternal."*

Will we simply say we trust God, or will we truly place our whole lives in His hands?

9. THE ULTIMATE TEST

When we claim to be disciples of the Lord Jesus Christ, is that because we have made some intellectual decision at some point in history to believe some truths about a man called Jesus? Or are we disciples of the Lord Jesus Christ because we have met Him; and we know Him; and we love Him; and we have a daily relationship with Him? When Jesus said, *"follow me"* did we say *"yes"* fully? Did we go all the way? Have we left everything in our hearts to follow Him? Or do we still have a tight grip on all those things that appear so precious at times? Is there anything that stands above our loyalty, our allegiance and our love for the Lord Jesus Christ?

We continue to face many tests each day whether we know them as tests or not. How are you going with them? Are you passing the submission test: to God; to your spouse; to your Pastor and leaders in the Church; to your boss at work; to every brother and sister in Christ? Are you passing the obedience test? Are you ignoring the clear guidelines that are laid down for us in the Bible as you go your own way, inviting Satan to inhabit your disobedience and bring pain and turmoil into your life and the lives of those around you?

Are you passing the servant test: making choices every day to serve the needs of others above your own? How about the giving test? Where is your time and effort and energy and money being directed? How easily do you forgive others? Are you making deliberate choices to bless others with your own abundance? And what about the trust test? In whom do you place your trust when things go wrong; when people or even friends turn on you; when you find yourself having to submit to people you disagree with? Do you really trust God in all those circumstances?

It is questions like these we have been confronting in the most practical possible way throughout this study, and I pray that you will spend time with this book in the days ahead and allow the Spirit of God to bring changes where they are needed. In this final chapter I want us to look at the ultimate test. This test sums up all the tests on the discipleship road. This test lies at the very heart of a fruitful relationship with Jesus.

> **Matthew 16:24-25** *Then Jesus said to his disciples, "Whoever wants to be my disciple must deny themselves and take up their cross and follow me. For whoever wants to save their life will lose it, but whoever loses their life for me will find it."*

It is so important that we understand just how literally Jesus meant these words. When Paul says we are united with Christ, he means in His life as well as His death, as well as His resurrection. The whole experience of Jesus becomes our experience, and so when we study the life and ministry of Jesus, we need to understand that we are seeing a model of the life of every Christian who seriously wants to follow Him. The dates and times and people and circumstances will all be different, but we can rightly expect to travel a similar road to Jesus if we decide to take this discipleship thing seriously. Jesus calls us to deny ourselves – which means we look away from ourselves and our own interests completely and choose to walk the path He walks.

We need to realise that the gospel account of the life and ministry of Jesus is far more than a history lesson. Yes, there is no doubt that this man walked the earth many years ago and did all those things and then He suffered and died on a cross and rose from the dead in three days. All of that is documented history. But the life and ministry and mission of Jesus is exactly the same today as it was back then.

Jesus continues to teach and heal and deliver and save. He continues to confront all the religious spirits and oppressive governments. He continues to suffer at the hands of godless men and women. He just does it through His spirit dwelling in you and me. That is all that has changed.

If you want a genuine, no-punches-pulled job description of a disciple, you just need to read the gospels and write down everything that Jesus did. I suggest that His final week on earth is the most important of all to study. We can learn a lot from that final week in the life of Jesus. The contrasts were incredible. From a hero on Palm Sunday to a deserted criminal a week later. It would have been very hard to deal with that shift emotionally - even for Jesus - but He was prepared. He knew Who He was. He knew where He was going. He knew the power of the One Who would get Him through it all.

If you and I understand the cost of following Jesus; if we are fully prepared for our Palm Sundays and our betrayals and denials, our Gethsemane's and our Calvary's - then as hard as it will still be to endure, we will make it through and see our stone rolled away and experience the power of our resurrection.

I fear that many of us are not prepared, however. I fear that when some of these things come against us, we fail to see the hand of God in them. We fail to see His refining power at work in our lives. We fail to accept that we are simply traveling the same road as the One we claim to follow. All too often in our walk with Jesus we get to Palm Sunday; we get to the fun time; we get to the point where everything is going so well - and we set up camp! We are happy for Jesus to keep going – that's His job – that's His calling and we don't need to go through all that.

Nothing could be further from the truth. If we are not prepared to follow Jesus all the way to Calvary then we will never know the power of the empty tomb. We will never fully know Jesus until we have made a choice to go where He goes and to feel what He feels and do what He does.

To understand the full measure of what it means to follow Jesus, we must recognize that discipleship is not just a call to learn from Jesus – it is a call to walk in His footsteps; to endure what He endured; love as He loved; and ultimately, to surrender as He surrendered.

Jesus does not invite us into this comfortable existence where we get to pick and choose which parts of His life we want Him to live through us. He calls us to follow Him completely, even to the point of laying down our lives for Him.

Jesus' journey to the cross was not an accident or a tragic end to an otherwise inspiring ministry. It was the very purpose for which He came. Throughout His time on earth, He repeatedly told His disciples that He would suffer, be rejected, and ultimately be killed before rising again (Mark 8:31). Yet, even with these warnings, they struggled to grasp the depth of His mission.

When Peter rebuked Jesus for predicting His own suffering, Jesus responded sharply: *"Get behind me, Satan! You do not have in mind the concerns of God, but merely human concerns"* (Mark 8:33). This moment highlights a crucial truth: to follow Jesus is to embrace God's plan, not our own. If we are only concerned with self-preservation, comfort, and success in this world, we will miss the very essence of being a disciple. True discipleship always means setting aside all our human concerns and boldly aligning ourselves with God's eternal purposes.

The words of Jesus above in Matthew 16:24-25 are radical. In His time, the cross was not a symbol of religious devotion but of shame, suffering, and death. When Jesus instructed His followers to take up their cross, He was calling them to suffer, to be rejected, and even to die for His sake.

To take up our cross means:

1. **Dying to self:** We no longer live for our desires, ambitions, or plans. Instead, we surrender all to Christ.

2. **Enduring hardship for the gospel:** Whether it be persecution, loss, or suffering, we embrace it as part of our calling.

3. **Living with an eternal perspective:** We no longer measure success by worldly standards but by faithfulness to God.

The ultimate test we face on this discipleship road involves surrendering everything. Following Jesus requires total surrender. The rich young ruler wanted to follow Jesus, but when confronted with the cost - selling all he had and giving to the poor - he walked away sorrowful (Matthew 19:16-22). Why? Because he valued his possessions more than he valued Christ. Each of us has something we must surrender to follow Jesus. It may not be wealth, but it could be our reputation, our comfort, our security, or even our relationships. Jesus made it clear that nothing should come before Him:

> **Matthew 10:37-38** *"Anyone who loves their father or mother more than me is not worthy of me; anyone who loves their son or daughter more than me is not worthy of me. Whoever does not take up their cross and follow me is not worthy of me."*

This is the ultimate test: have we truly submitted to the Lordship of Jesus in every area of our lives? Have we placed Him above everything else? Jesus never sugar-coated the cost of following Him. He warned that His followers would be hated, persecuted, and even killed for His name's sake. The Apostle Paul understood this only too well. He suffered many beatings, imprisonment, shipwrecks, and countless hardships for the sake of Christ (2 Corinthians 11:23-28). Yet, he counted it all as nothing compared to knowing Jesus:

> **Philippians 3:8** *"I consider everything a loss because of the surpassing worth of knowing Christ Jesus my Lord, for whose sake I have lost all things. I consider them garbage, that I may gain Christ."*

Paul understood that true discipleship means nothing in this world can compare to Christ. He lived and died for that truth. So what does this mean for us? Most of us may never be called to physically die for our faith, but we are called to live as though we have already died to ourselves. Here are a few practical ways you can do that:

1. **Daily surrender:** Each day, choose to put Christ first in your decisions, actions, and relationships.

2. **Endure hardship with faith:** When trials come, see them as opportunities to trust God and grow in Him.

3. **Be bold in your witness:** Do not be ashamed of Christ. Share the gospel, even when it's uncomfortable.

4. **Love sacrificially:** Serve others selflessly, just as Christ did.

5. **Keep your eyes on eternity:** Remember that this life is temporary, but our reward in Christ is eternal.

Even though discipleship is costly, the reward is far, far greater. Jesus promised that those who lose their lives for His sake will find true life. Our suffering is temporary. Our sacrifices are momentary. But the reward is eternal.

> **Mark 10:29-30** *"Truly I tell you," Jesus replied, "no one who has left home or brothers or sisters or mother or father or children or fields for me and the gospel will fail to receive a hundred times as much in this present age: homes, brothers, sisters, mothers, children and fields - along with persecutions - and in the age to come eternal life."*

As we conclude this study in discipleship, I leave you with this one simple question:

Will you go all the way with Jesus?

Not just part of the way; not just when it's easy; but all the way to the cross? Too many believers stop at Palm Sunday, enjoying the praise and the excitement but refusing to walk the road to Calvary. But Jesus calls us beyond that. He calls us to follow Him through all the suffering, through the trials, through the surrender, until we experience the resurrection power of God in our lives.

If we truly want to be His disciples, we must lay everything down and follow Him with all our hearts. The road can be difficult, but the destination is glorious. Jesus has gone before us, and He walks with us every day. May we be found faithful until the very end. Yes, Jesus endured the cross. For the joy set before Him - He went all the way. He trusted the Father to bring good out of His death. Because of Jesus' willingness to go all the way, salvation came to all mankind. God used His pain and His death to be a blessing to others. God will do that same for you and me. He wants us to give our life as Jesus gave His.

For some of us that will one day be literally true if we serve the Lord in an environment where our life is threatened because of our faith. But for all of us it is true every day in spiritual terms as we die to this world and to our own desires and pleasures and submit to the way of Jesus.

During a time of great struggle in my ministry many years ago, I went to see a Pastor friend of mine and shared my heart with him. When I had said all that I could say, he paused, then he said these words:

> *"Robert, I believe the Lord has prepared many wonderful resurrections for you in your life and ministry, but you will never experience the power of a resurrection if you have refused to die first. Death always precedes resurrection. You need to give up completely, in the flesh, and let your death lead you to the other side of this painful chapter in your life. Jesus will be with you every step – He has been there already – He knows the way – you just need to trust Him."*

That was a life-transforming visit with my brother in the Lord, and it has been my desire to help every disciple to learn what I learned that day and listen to what Jesus says:

> *"Follow Me, every day in every way; as I heal, deliver and raise from the dead; as I face the torment and pain of an execution; when people praise Me and give Me glory for what I do in their lives and when I lay on My face in the dust of Gethsemane begging the Father to end My suffering; when thousands respond to the truth I bring and success surrounds Me at every point; when most of My closest friends dessert Me as I breathe My last breath on the crooked cross … then, and only then, will we walk out of that tomb together, ready to meet the next challenge that comes our way."*

Will you follow Jesus - all the way - every day?

www.ingramcontent.com/pod-product-compliance
Lightning Source LLC
Chambersburg PA
CBHW071242020426
42333CB00015B/1593